ANY COMPLAINTS?
BLAME GOD!

ANY COMPLAINTS? BLAME GOD!

God's Message for Today – Habakkuk the Prophet Speaks

Martin Goldsmith

MILTON KEYNES ● COLORADO SPRINGS ● HYDERABAD

14 13 12 11 10 09 08   7 6 5 4 3 2 1

First published 2008 by Authentic Media
9 Holdom Avenue, Bletchley, Milton Keynes, Bucks, MK1 1QR, UK
1820 Jet Stream Drive, Colorado Springs, CO 80921, USA
OM Authentic Media, Medchal Road, Jeedimetla Village,
Secunderabad 500 055, A.P., India
www.authenticmedia.co.uk
Authentic Media is a division of IBS-STL U.K., limited by guarantee, with its
Registered Office at Kingstown Broadway, Carlisle, Cumbria CA3 0HA.
Registered in England & Wales No. 1216232. Registered charity 270162

British Library Cataloguing in Publication Data
A catalogue record for this book is available from the
British Library
ISBN-13: 978-1-85078-812-6

Cover Design by David Smart
Print Management by Adare
Printed in the UK by CPI Bookmarque, Croydon, CR0 4TD

Contents

Foreword   vii
Introduction   xiii

1 Habakkuk's First Complaint –
   Why Doesn't God Do Something   1

2 God's Shocking Answer –
   I Am Using the Babylonians   22

3 Habakkuk's Second Complaint –
   God, You Can't Do That!   37

4 How Will God Answer? –
   Though It Seems Slow, Wait for It!   57

5 God's Solution – God's Justice Prevails   75

6 Filled With the Knowledge of His Glory –
   Nothing To Complain About   91

7 A Song of Praise – Glory, Not Grumbling   103

Bibliography   123
Endnotes   126

Foreword

What a privilege it was as a theological student to sit at the feet of one of the top Bible expositors in the country! As a young man I revelled in Old Testament lectures from Alec Motyer, working with him through various Bible texts in the Hebrew. Under his inspiring teaching I discovered something of the riches of the book of Habakkuk. Its message is so simple and clear, but wonderfully profound at the same time.

It still remains highly relevant today. We are often tempted to look on life with the opposite of rose-tinted glasses, so that we see the dark side of everything. British culture in particular is fundamentally negative, and we always seem to be able to find something to complain about. In this pessimistic atmosphere, it sounds strange if we confess that we are enjoying life. Even if we have nothing more serious to complain about, there is always the weather: too hot or too cold, too wet or too dry!

Today we live in what is commonly called a 'blame society'. Whatever happens to us, we feel we have the right to blame someone else and perhaps look for compensation. For example, some legal companies encourage us to sue if we have had an accident at work, or suffered a fall on uneven pavement. It seems as though we can no longer take full responsibility for our own actions, but must find someone else to blame. So often, this 'someone else' is God. If serious sickness comes upon us or some other major suffering, it is God who we blame. Sometimes one feels a bit sorry for God! He seems to carry the can whenever anything goes wrong. Too often, people are slow to lay the blame on their own sin or their own failure. God is even considered to be personally responsible if natural disaster hits some area of the world. Any complaints? Blame God!

In more recent days I have seen again how an Old Testament prophet can speak into our lives personally and into the issues of contemporary society. It has been a privilege to be invited to speak in many conferences around the world and in several I have sought to expound the book of Habakkuk. The feedback has been so encouraging that it has stimulated me to try to put pen to paper, or rather fingers to computer. I am duly grateful to students at the All Nations Christian College 'Refresh for Mission' course, as well as to Norwegian Lutheran missionaries at the Bible Seminary of Fjellhaug in Oslo, guests at a holiday week with MasterSun and various others. Their enthusiasm has provided the stimulus God has used to inspire me to write.

Many Christians find reading the Old Testament a mixed experience which can be both fascinating and daunting. The exciting stories of the patriarchs, Jonah, Daniel and Ruth hold us all spellbound. The Psalms inspire us devotionally and such books as Proverbs challenge us in the fundamentals of daily living. But reading the prophets may make us feel like lost travellers struggling through a huge desert. Mile after mile of arid wilderness is occasionally relieved by the oasis of a golden verse which we can take as a clear Messianic prophecy of Jesus, or by a wonderful promise which we can apply to ourselves in our relationship with God. But often these nuggets remain separated from their textual context and from their historical significance at the time when the prophet was writing.

When people begin to understand the relatively short and easy book of Habakkuk in its context and relate it to our day, then it can form a peg on which to hang the other longer and more difficult prophets like Isaiah, Jeremiah and Ezekiel. This is equally true of the other so-called 'minor prophets'. Working as a missionary in Indonesia among the local churches there, I sometimes found it helpful to teach about Habakkuk as an intro-duction to a wider understanding of the prophets. Through this, Christians began to feed themselves bibli-cally as they delved further into the Old Testament in general and the prophets in particular.

Although Habakkuk is such a small book with only three short chapters; fifty-six verses in all, nevertheless it contains several well-known 'golden verses'. In explain-ing evangelistically the basic outline of the Gospel peo-ple often use Habakkuk 1:13, 'Your eyes are too pure to look on evil; you cannot tolerate wrong'. This has been used widely to show that God in his absolute burning purity cannot tolerate anything imperfect. Sin separates humanity from the God of holiness, so no relationship between God and sinful human beings is possible. But the Gospel with its good news of Jesus' sacrificial death for our sin allows God to remain entirely just and blame-less in his judgment and yet also to justify repentant sin-ners (Rom. 3:26). Through the cross of Jesus we can be reconciled to the holy God whose eyes are otherwise too pure to look on us with all our imperfection.

Another 'golden verse' is found in Habakkuk 2:4. 'The righteous will live by . . . faith' became the watchword and foundation of the Reformation, and of evangelical life and faith. Romans 1:17 and Galatians 3:11, direct quotes from Habakkuk, are frequently used to demonstrate that we can never approach God on the basis of our own merit or good works, but only by God's grace received through faith alone. As we shall see when we look at Habakkuk 2:4 later in this book, we will find in Hebrews 10:38 a different understanding of this verse which is actually nearer to Habakkuk's original meaning. Sometimes as Christians we fail to give the same emphasis to the use of this verse from Habakkuk in Hebrews 10:38, emphasizing rather its use in Romans and Galatians. How we understand these words in Romans, Galatians or Hebrews will depend partly on our understanding of Habakkuk 2:4 in its context.

A further oasis and relief in what may feel like the prophetic desert comes in Habakkuk 2:14: 'The earth will be filled with the knowledge of the glory of the Lord, as the waters cover the sea.' This key missionary text inspired our forefathers to sacrificial ministry and hope 'aimed at hastening that day when the earth will be filled with the knowledge of the glory of the Lord'.[1] May we today walk in their footsteps with the same missionary zeal and expectant hope! As we revel in the joy of this sure promise of God, we will surely exchange the blame culture for one of rejoicing and praise.

Habakkuk 3:2, with its passionate prayer for renewal, is often linked to Habakkuk 3:19 in Christians' longing for the reviving work of the Holy Spirit: 'The Sovereign Lord is my strength, he makes my feet like the feet of a deer, he enables me to go on the heights'. We thirst for such an outpouring of the Spirit that the Lord's mighty works of old may be renewed in our time and in our nations. And for ourselves we earnestly desire that God would make our feet 'like the feet of a deer' and that he would endow us with his strength to be able to walk nimbly on the heights of trial and danger, through the ups and downs of our daily lives. Even in such situations we want to continue with a positive note of praise.

As we approach the book of Habakkuk, let us pray that God by his Spirit would speak to us not only through the 'nuggets', but also through the whole book in its context. No longer do we want the word of God in the Old Testament to be like a desert stretching interminably and incomprehensibly before us. Let the prophetic word speak!

Introduction

Who was Habakkuk?

We know virtually nothing about who Habakkuk was, what his family background may have been, or anything about his ministry beyond the prophetic message he has left us.

His name has traditionally been thought to relate to a term meaning 'to embrace', perhaps underlining the ministry of the prophet in embracing and thus comforting his people in the midst of traumatic times. So Luther paralleled Habakkuk's ministry to someone embracing a child who is hurt and crying. We may blame God for our trials, but actually he is longing to enfold us in the warmth of his comforting arms. Certainly this little prophetic book has proved a means of comfort to people facing the inexplicable mystery of suffering.

More recently the name 'Habakkuk' has been thought to come from an Akkadian plant name.[1] But this too is debatable. In any case, we have to admit that his name gives us little clue as to who Habakkuk really was.

There is just one interesting pointer to Habakkuk's identity. In Habakkuk 1:1 and 3:1 the title 'prophet' is added to his name. These two verses are the only occasions when Habakkuk's name appears and in both cases the title is added, so evidently this is a significant element in his identity.

There were two sorts of prophets. We read of official prophetic bodies called 'the sons of the prophets' (1 Kgs. 20:35), to which the 'procession of prophets' in 1 Samuel 10:5,10 doubtless also belonged. Then there were also individual prophets who were especially called to proclaim the word of the Lord to his people. For example, Amos insisted that he was 'neither a prophet nor a prophet's son' (Amos 7:14), but was particularly called from his work as a shepherd and carer of sycamore-fig trees to bring God's prophetic message to Israel. We may speculate that the title 'the prophet' added to Habakkuk's name in those two verses would indicate that he belonged to the recognized body of prophets. He would therefore be accepted officially as a prophet in the community.

The dating of Habakkuk's prophecy

The message of Habakkuk clearly relates closely to the movements of history which were unfolding before his eyes. Habakkuk evidently had a firm faith in the belief that God rules over everything that happens. God is the sovereign Lord of history. What occurs among the nations is not by chance, or merely by the power of political and military rulers. God himself is in control. Of course, this truth leaves him open to criticism when things seem to go wrong, but actually he sees the end from the beginning, and the ultimate goal of God's purposes is perfect.

God cannot be sidelined into just 'spiritual' issues, for he is Lord of all. Nothing is outside his absolute authority. What a comfort to us in the twenty-first century, as we face the potential tragedies of global warming and ecological disaster, the traumas of human history, the madness of wars and violence, and evil rife in nation after nation. Whatever we may think, God's grace will prevail.

Considerable debate has raged concerning the historical context in which Habakkuk was writing and from which he sees God's message to his people. To some extent our understanding of prophecy generally influences this question. Some more liberal commentators deny the possibility of any prophecy which foretells what will happen in the future. With that view of prophecy they declare that Habakkuk must have been writing *after* the rise to power of the Babylonians (also referred to as the Chaldeans) which is so evidently the context of his prophecy (e.g. Hab. 1:6).

At the other end of the spectrum, some strongly conservative scholars believe that biblical prophecy must be foreseeing things that lie beyond the current horizons of history, unseen in the future. While this reaffirms Christian faith in a God who is able to work miraculously, it goes against Habakkuk's emphasis that his prophetic message is based on what he actually *sees*.

A more balanced view may be that the Babylonians were already gaining strength but had not yet achieved the pinnacle of power, and it is at this time that Habakkuk is writing. So Kenneth Barker and Waylon Bailey[2] declare that 'the almost consensus view sees the wicked in Judah itself . . . and sees the Chaldeans as the instrument of the Lord to punish the wicked'. We may doubt whether this is actually 'the almost consensus view' but nevertheless agree with their historical understanding of the backdrop to Habakkuk's prophecy.

How then can we determine when Habakkuk was writing? Habakkuk's description of Judah's sin in 1:2–4

reflects not only a sense of God's hatred of all evil, but
would seem also to have within it a deep disillusionment
and disappointment. Perhaps the prophet really expected God's people to be demonstrating the glory of God
in holiness. After all, this was God's purpose in calling
Israel to be his people. From the time of Abraham's call
in Genesis 12:1–3 God clearly intended that Israel should
so demonstrate the glory and holiness of God in her
national life that the surrounding Gentile nations would
be drawn in, like bees to honey or moths to the light, to
worship the God of Israel. But Habakkuk was deeply
aware that God's perfect aims were not being fulfilled –
and he duly complained bitterly to God.

We may wonder therefore whether Habakkuk had in
recent years been buoyed up by a time of reformation in
Israel, but was now saddened that disastrous wickedness still remained in Judah despite the reformation. Or
had Judah slipped back into rebellion and the reformation dried up? In our times many in the countries of
Europe are also deeply saddened as they contemplate
the sinful nature of their nations and societies. Has God
lost control of the world? This question troubles the
minds of many people.

We know that the rediscovery of the Book of the Law
under Josiah in 622/1 BC (2 Chr. 34:14–33) and the godly
zeal of good King Josiah[3] led to just such a reformation in
Judah. But it would seem that Josiah's reforming rule
had only destroyed the outward forms of idolatry without changing the hearts and desires of the people. The
revival came from the king, but apparently did not affect
the population more generally. It is perhaps significant
that Habakkuk's denunciation of Judah in 1:2–4 casti-
gates their violence, wickedness and perverted law, but
it does not mention anything about idolatry or religious
sin. Does this reflect the situation under Josiah where the

outward forms of heathen worship had all been destroyed by the king, but social and relational corruption still prevailed among the people?

If so, it would seem that Habakkuk may well have been writing some time after the reformation issuing out of 622/1 BC. We also have to allow some years before Habakkuk would have become disillusioned and disappointed that the renewal had proved superficial, hardly touching ordinary people or society at large.

In modern Europe too Christians repeatedly find their hope aroused by some new revival movement, but after a while become disillusioned as it fails to touch the wider public and gradually withers away.

Habakkuk declares that God's 'raising up the Babylonians' (1:6) would amaze the people of Judah (1:5). Clearly the Babylonians were not yet a major force in the history of the area. And yet their rapacious ferocity is described by the prophet as something people would know. So their military campaigns en route to regional power must have begun.[4] The rise of the Babylonians started with Nabopolassar coming to the throne of Babylon in 626 BC. In 612 BC the Babylonians actually captured Nineveh, the capital city of the Assyrian empire, to which the northern kingdom of Israel had been carried captive in the previous century. Then, in 605 BC, Babylon defeated the Egyptians under Pharaoh Neco at the momentous battle of Carchemish. So the Babylonians gained control of the whole Middle East as far as the borders of Egypt. In 609 BC, in the early days of this military campaign, Habakkuk's king, Josiah, was tragically killed. Judah now became a vassal of the Babylonians, suffering considerable devastation.[5]

It would seem that Habakkuk must have been writing some time before the Babylonians gained power over the whole region in 605 BC,[6] but after they had begun to rival the Assyrians and also some years after the outbreak of Josiah's reformation in Judah in 622/1 BC. Many have dated Habakkuk's prophecy to between the death of Josiah in 609 BC and Babylon's great victory in 605 BC. However, Habakkuk assumed that the rise of the Babylonians would come as a surprise to his audience. This seems to indicate that he was writing even before the capture of Nineveh in 612 BC. So we may hazard a guess that Habakkuk's prophecy can be dated somewhere around 615 BC. But we cannot be too dogmatic about this assumption, for even evangelical scholars differ widely despite their agreement concerning the fundamental nature of prophecy.

Habakkuk's Prophecy

We can divide the book of Habakkuk into clear sections in order to examine it closely. Habakkuk 1:1–4 is the prophet's first complaint, and 1:5–11 reveals God's shocking answer. 1:12–17 covers Habakkuk's second complaint, followed by a time of waiting in 2:1–4. God presents his solution in 2:5–20, and in 2:14 makes it clear there is nothing to complain about. The prophet ends in 3:1–19 with a song of praise and prayer.

Each chapter will cover one section of the book of Habakkuk, and we will begin with Habakkuk's first complaint: why doesn't God do something?

One

Habakkuk's First Complaint – Why Doesn't God Do Something?

Habakkuk 1:1–4

From the outset of his prophecy Habakkuk looks out on a world in which sin seems to have taken control. His nation had turned away from the worship of the living God. Iniquity of every sort stared him in the face and he felt a deep sense of despair. There seemed to be no hope of revival and restoration of true worship and righteousness. People had sunk too deeply into sin. Why didn't God do something to put this situation right?

Many of us today find ourselves in a similar predicament. Our nation seems to have rejected the Lord and sin has become accepted as normal in everyday life. The church and the people of God seem impotent in the face of governments, media and educational patterns which appear literally hell-bent in their pursuit of agendas which deny the sovereignty of God and which push faith in him to the sidelines of life. And God seems to just twiddle his thumbs.

That is the context into which Habakkuk's prophecy speaks. It is highly relevant for us today.

'The oracle that Habakkuk the prophet received'

What was this oracle that Habakkuk the prophet received? The Hebrew word which we have here translated as 'oracle' is *massa*. This is a word rich with meaning. Generally in the Old Testament the word *massa* carries the sense of something which is a definite burden. It is a load which must be carried. W.C. Kaiser[1] asserts that the word refers to prophetic threats or words heavy with doom. Such threatening words of divine judgment lie heavily on the heart and mind of the prophet, so that the old Authorised Version translation 'burden' would seem to convey the true sense of this word.

In the prophets *massa* commonly carries the sense of a divine word which causes deep unease because of the fearful nature of judgment at the hands of a holy God. Thus it is used by Isaiah in his series of denunciations against the various nations – the burden of Moab, Damascus, Egypt and so on (Is. 15; 17; 19). The frightening messages of God through Nahum and Malachi also begin with the declaration that they are conveying a 'burden' which can only cause the messenger and his listeners to shiver with apprehension and fear. And the word occurs frequently with this clear sense of a 'burden' in the other prophets as well.

So Habakkuk affirms right at the outset of his prophecy that his message touches his heart and causes him deep emotional concern. It was a burden to him. Why then does he feel it weighs so heavily upon him? Again and again in the Old Testament the true prophetic message pronounces God's uncompromising demand for holiness, both in individual personal living and also in social justice and righteousness. Prophecy announces God's judgment against sin, whether it is within Israel as the covenant people of God, or among the heathen nations surrounding them.

This true biblical prophecy contrasts sharply with much modern prophecy, which often just encourages the people of God that they are very special in God's eyes and lie at the centre of God's loving purposes.

The Hebrew word *massa* is also sometimes understood to mean an oracle of judgment against foreign nations.[2] This understanding certainly fits the context of the whole book of Habakkuk, which clearly contains a divine word of judgment against the oppressive Babylonians. The NIV translation 'oracle' would seem to be supported by Proverbs 30:1 and 31:1, where the sense is of a word from God, but this translation has no thought of judgment against the Gentile nations surrounding Israel. *Massa* reminds us of the wonderful truth that our God is one who communicates with his people; he is a God who speaks. Sometimes his message brings comfort, sometimes it warns us of the dangers of God's holy anger against all sin.

Surprisingly, in the light of the basic sense of *massa* as a burden, the word has yet another twist in its significance in 1 Chronicles 15:22,27 where joyful praise and singing accompany the return of the ark of the covenant to its rightful place. Here the NIV gives the translation 'singing', a sung message of praise and worship inspired by God himself. Israel brought up the ark 'with shouts, with the sounding of rams' horns and trumpets, and of cymbals, and the playing of lyres and harps' (1 Chr. 15:28). King David was so filled with rejoicing that he danced in celebration (1 Chr. 15:29).

As Christians we too are called to times of exuberant and even uninhibited joy before the Lord. And we have greater cause to rejoice than just the return of the ark of the covenant!

Nevertheless, the context of the overall message in Habakkuk would seem to argue against this understanding of the word *massa*. Habakkuk does not see his message as a cause for rejoicing, but rather it burdens him with a heavy load. When we are heavily burdened with the tragic circumstances all around us, Habakkuk gives us an example of unburdening our hearts and laying the whole situation honestly before God.

In our generation and situations too we need to allow God's word to move us emotionally to a deep sense of awe. Our hearts need to become troubled by the divine threat of judgment. We dare not take the sin of our contemporary societies for granted. We can easily become so accustomed to the evils around us that we are no longer greatly concerned by them. And in our desire to emphasize the grace and love of a forgiving God we may underplay his holy wrath and the reality of his judgment against sin. But when we communicate with God, we need to be realistic about what is going on.

We may sometimes lose sight of the possibility of a society in which the love of God reigns supreme. In the East Malaysian revival in the 1970s, the whole population of one area of Sarawak was converted and revived through a glorious movement of the Holy Spirit. The headmaster of the local school used to declare with joy how pleasurable it now was to teach. The teachers no longer had to worry about discipline in class, for all the children had become revived followers of Jesus. Likewise it was no longer necessary to lock one's house when going out.

I remember leaving my suitcase in the middle of the airport hall with my camera lying loose on top. After a couple of days I returned to find my suitcase and camera still safely there. On my case lay a pile of little brown envelopes as well as various bags of rice and fruit. To my amazement, the envelopes contained thank-offerings for my teaching. It was enough to cover my return airfare from London and all my expenses while in Malaysia! In a Christian revival situation both camera and money could lie unguarded in the airport hall without fear of theft.

As we remember God's ideal purpose for his people, we can only weep when we see the consequences of the sin which prevails all around us. What a waste of money and resources in having to provide endless security guards, CCTV cameras, locks and lights! Revival would bring economic as well as spiritual transformation.

So it was with Habakkuk. What he saw in Israel had become a burden on his heart, and he openly lays his complaints on the altar before the Lord. May it be so with us too!

'Received'

In normal life we assume that oracles consist of words which are to be heard. Messages and prophecies are to be received with open *ears*. But Habakkuk, as is common in the Bible, underlines the importance of open *eyes*. The Hebrew word translated 'received' actually means 'saw'. So Habakkuk receives the prophetic message from God by seeing what is happening all around him. God's word is not only heard, but is also particularly *seen*.

Thus a prophet in the Old Testament is commonly called a 'seer', one whose eyes are open to *see* the word of God. If we want to discern what God is saying to us and to our generation, we need to observe carefully what is happening in the world today. The more we can learn of what God is doing both in our own country and around the world, the more we shall appreciate how he wants to direct our lives and the life of our church. That is the clue to finding God's answer to our complaints.

David Ben-Gurion, the first Prime Minister of the new state of Israel, asserts that a prophet is 'no oracle. He isn't clairvoyant except through the exercise of his intelligence.' He further comments that the biblical prophets were 'men of the world concerned with the daily facts of life in relation to their understanding of God's will.'[3]

It is an interesting cultural phenomenon that Jews and Arabs have traditionally prayed with their eyes open. Does this signify that they are coming to God in prayer whilst being aware of all that is happening around them? They come into God's presence together with all the people in their vicinity and in the context of whatever is going on. They are not approaching God in prayer in isolation from other people or from surrounding events. In contrast, Europeans have traditionally come to God in prayer with eyes firmly shut, with the intention that they may be able personally and individually to concentrate on prayer without distraction.

Of course, it is not of biblical significance whether our eyes are physically open or shut when we pray – that is just a small cultural difference. But we have to ask more fundamental questions concerning our approach to God in prayer. Does this cultural distinction arise from the individualism of European life, whereas Semitic cultures are much more communal? And are the events going on around us as we pray merely distractions, or are they the context of our prayer and of our prophetic ministry?

Christians today may pray with their eyes open or closed, but all of us need to be deeply aware of what God is doing in the world today. As we shall see again and again through the prophecy of Habakkuk, God is the Lord of history and therefore what happens in the world stems ultimately from him. There can be no line drawn between so-called 'secular' politics, social, environmental or economic matters and the more 'spiritual' matters of prayer, mission and church life. Our God is Lord of all.

Clearly, then, in Habakkuk considerable emphasis is given to what the prophet sees. Already within the first five verses he uses three different verbs for 'to see'[4] and in 1:1 the 'oracle' or 'burden' is not only 'received' (NIV), but is actually seen with the eyes.

Habakkuk's First Complaint (1:2–4)

These verses describe the tragic situation which faced the prophet as he looked out upon the world around him. Sin and evil appeared to reign unhindered with all their fearful consequences in people's daily lives. And sadly many of us today in our modern world will find that Habakkuk's situation rings alarm bells, for we too live in similar societies.

In his prayer to God Habakkuk lists some of the prevailing evils of his day, and what a frightening parade they form. 'Violence' (twice), 'injustice', 'wrong', 'destruction', 'strife', 'conflict', the law paralysed, justice never prevailing and indeed perverted, the wicked hemming in the righteous. What a catalogue! What a recipe for disaster! And for Habakkuk the prophet it is frighteningly clear that such sin can only lead to divine judgment, for God is holy and cannot tolerate such obvious evil.

'Violence'

The repetition of this word (*hamas*) in verses two and three underlines the fact that violence is the evil which underlies the whole situation of Israel at that time. In *The Brown–Driver–Briggs Hebrew and English Lexicon*, the

Hebrew *hamas* is defined with words like 'rude wickedness' and 'noisy, wild ruthlessness'. It includes the idea
of seizing what one wants by means of such unbridled
force that one rides roughshod over others. Violence
never even considers what it does to other people. For
example, a Chinese lady from Hong Kong recently
shared with me her sense of shock on coming to Britain.
She felt that people showed so little regard for others.

Other parts of the Bible show how violence is end-
emic to fallen human nature. In Genesis 6:11,13 violence
filled the earth in the days of Noah. Genesis connects
violence with 'corruption', for it destroys the very God-
given nature of the created order. God's purposes for the
world and for humanity are spoiled and radically
changed by violence, so that the whole earth contradicts
the very character of God in his beauty and holiness.
Don't blame God! It is men and women who push grace
and love aside in favour of power-driven violence.

As O. Palmer Robertson points out,[5] there is a clear
parallel between Job 19:7 and Habakkuk 1:2. In Job also
we read, 'I cry out "Violence!" and you do not answer.'
And in Job too violence goes hand-in-hand with injustice. Job's God-given life of peace and harmony has been
rudely shattered. His friends and even his wife and family stand against him (Job 19:17–19). God's ideals for
human life and relationships have been shattered. In Job
it becomes clear that Satan himself is the origin of such
violence. But why does God not demonstrate that he is
victorious over the Devil?

Such fundamental corruption of God's loving purposes
by the indiscriminate use of force is seen by various
prophets to be a basic human problem. Again and again
they speak out against such violence, condemning it and
all who engage in it. Such violence is seen not only in
direct actions, but also in immoderate words and attitudes

of abuse and animosity. Undisciplined verbal attacks can harm people just as much as actual physical aggression. As Christians we should thoroughly dislike the aggressive and ill-tempered interpersonal relationships which are so often portrayed on television. This angry lack of self-control in the use of words forms the backdrop for active physical violence. And the prophets warn repeatedly that violence can only lead to God's judgment.

As we read on in the Old Testament history, we note that their words are fulfilled. Israel is destroyed by alien nations and taken captive to exile in Babylon. Habakkuk too foresees the ferociously cruel invasion of the Babylonians as the outworking of God's holy judgment against the sin of Judah. But in his spirit he hates what God seems to be doing.

One notable aspect of violence is that it is often practised against the weak and vulnerable. Jeremiah declares the command of the Lord to 'do what is just and right'. This particularly includes the injunction to 'do no wrong or violence to the alien, the fatherless or the widow' (Jer. 22:3). When violence goes unchecked in society, it is generally the defenceless who suffer most. But the Bible declares to us that God has a particular concern for those who are vulnerable – the people who have no one to protect them. As the people of God, it is incumbent on us to care particularly for the powerless and underprivileged in our societies, the misfits and the unpopular, the handicapped and the poor.

'Injustice'

In Habakkuk 1:3 we see the Hebrew word *awen*. Herbert Livingston accuses biblical theologians of having 'given little attention to *awen* as a contributor to the understanding of sin'.[6] In the Authorised Version translation of the Bible *awen* is most commonly translated as 'iniquity'. Livingston shows that 'the primary meaning of the word seems to have two facets: either that of trouble which leads on to wickedness, or an emphasis on emptiness which moves on to idolatry'.

Readers of the NIV may note that the translation 'injustice' is unfortunate. Habakkuk would appear to be referring rather to a more general state, in which people feel troubled and empty in their lives. They therefore indulge in all sorts of iniquity and particularly in idolatry. God is removed from his central position in the world, and replaced by various other things or activities which become idols in people's lives.[7] Such idolatry not only stems from a kind of emptiness in life, but also results in further emptiness as a consequence. How clearly we see this all around us today! It should be a burden on our souls, as it was on Habakkuk.

We notice again Habakkuk's emphasis on what he sees with his eyes. He complains that God is causing him to *see* this iniquity and idolatry.[8] Even the evil which the prophet sees is part of God's word to and through Habakkuk. Are we today alert to what God is saying through the evil that we see around us? Although this sin is part of God's message to Habakkuk, it nevertheless causes him deep concern. It is one ingredient in his 'burden' (1:1).

Struggling under the weight of this burden, Habakkuk cries out to God, 'why do you make me look at injustice? Why do you tolerate wrong?' (1:3). It has been suggested that Habakkuk's question 'implies that God's inactivity had allowed wicked people to dominate Judah'.[9] Certainly the text may be viewed in this way. But it could also just mean what it says, namely that God caused the prophet to see what was happening all around him. It was God who opened Habakkuk's eyes to observe the situation and to note its significance. Surely for any prophetic ministry we need to ask God to open our eyes to observe world events and also what is going on within our own nation and people. Then we need to allow what we see to become a deep burden on our hearts. A prophetic ministry is no easy option! But at least we can follow the example of the prophet and unburden our heavy hearts in the presence of God.

'Wrong'

As is common in the pattern of Hebrew poetry, the two questions in the first half of verse three belong together. The second question parallels the first, adding an extra nuance to it. So it is that iniquity and 'wrong' are often found together.

The Hebrew word for 'wrong' (*amal*) carries the idea of something that is grievous and toilsome. It is used for example in Isaiah 53:11, where it is prophesied that the Servant shall endure 'the suffering [AV 'travail'] of his soul'. When people slip into iniquity and idolatry, there is not only the inevitable consequence of heaviness of soul. Work also begins to become burdensome and one loses the sense of joy and privilege in one's work. It then becomes a labour which stands in marked contrast to the creational purpose of God. In the Garden of Eden Adam and Eve looked after the garden with ease and pleasure in an assured familiar relationship with God himself. But as a result of their fall into sin the ground was cursed, and it would only be 'through painful toil' that they would gain access to the earth's produce (Gen. 3:17). Drudgery and toil would replace light-hearted pleasure and nobility of work.

A further by-product of such unfulfilling labour is commonly associated with this word 'wrong'. It carries the sense of 'grievance'. As Habakkuk looks at the people around him, he is saddened to observe the burdensome round of labour which can only cause a sense of bitterness. Life had become a daily grind of toil, in which it had lost its sparkle. Living under the curse of sin and godlessness will generally lead to such burdensome meaninglessness. This may be seen today in European societies where God has been dethroned. And in its turn it leads to an atmosphere of blame.

Habakkuk is deeply saddened to see his neighbours living in such a way. And he finds it incomprehensible how God can 'tolerate' such evil. How can God stand it when he sees people living in such iniquity? If the sight of such evil is a pain to a mere human like Habakkuk, how much more must it hurt God himself in all his purity and righteousness?

'Destruction and violence', 'strife' and 'conflict'

While 'violence' stood on its own in verse two, now it is joined together with 'destruction'. Similarly, in 2:17 'violence' and 'destruction' combine to deliver a message of devastation and ruin. This combination is found also in other prophets.[10] Destruction and chaos are the inevitable consequences of violence whether in society generally, or more particularly in a home and family.

Indeed, history would support the prophets in showing how godless iniquity will be followed by the tragic sequel of violence and ruin. Where the standards of God are replaced by naked power, chaos easily prevails. The atheistic Communist experiment has demonstrated this to a significant degree. With revolution coming 'out of the barrel of a gun', violence formed the very foundation of the new society. Communist Party power became the basis for the development of their country. At lower levels in society and in daily life ordinary people sought to exercise power over others, but this led to the ultimate breakdown and destruction of the nation.

In Britain today there is also a danger that people can only get their way by the use of power or even force. Governments will listen to those who exercise violence. Loud demonstrations or violence on the streets force authorities to pay attention. The authorities are tempted to seek peace and harmony by appeasing these factions, while those who use more peaceful and democratic means can find that their voice remains unheeded. Habakkuk was witnessing something of this nature in the Judah of his day.

The prophet goes on to link destruction and violence with 'strife' and 'conflict'. He observes how relationships have broken down. Our relationships form the bedrock of life and society. African theologians have underlined this reality, stressing that we only attain true personality when we are in relationship with others. The philosopher Martin Buber likewise emphasized the vital importance of our being in 'I-Thou' relationships rather than just 'I-It'. But this emphasis also goes right back to the teaching of Augustine, who saw the need for relationships of love, as exemplified to perfection in the Trinity. More recently Karl Barth in his *Church Dogmatics* has also underlined the Trinity as the basis for community as opposed to singular individualism.[11]

In the glorious reality of the Trinity we see the ideal of relationships. Each Person retains their particular identity and yet there is a perfect unity in diversity. This unity is expressed in absolute harmony, both of being and of purpose. And all three Persons delight in love to serve each other. Thus the Holy Spirit constantly points away from himself to glorify and exalt the Son, Jesus Christ. But Jesus' goal is always to obey and glorify the Father, doing his will rather than his own. Jesus is the way to the Father, revealing him to us. Then the Father is shown in John's Gospel to have the ministry of glorifying the Son (Jn. 17:1,4) while ultimately the Son will lay everything at the feet of the Father so that God the Father 'may be all in all' (1 Cor. 15:28). What a model of loving unity and humble service of each other! In the Trinity we are given the perfect ideal pattern for true relationships at every level – in the home, at work, in the church, in wider society, in political structures and in international relationships.

But Habakkuk saw just the opposite in Judah. Strife and conflict ruled the day. No wonder he was burdened by what he saw! Today, too, Christians need to share the prophet's sense of burden as we look out on a world dominated by destruction and violence, strife and conflict. Let us not become hardened to the harsh realities around us just because they have become so commonplace!

'The law is paralysed', 'justice never prevails' and is 'perverted'

So we come to the climax of the evil which surrounded the prophet and which was such a burden upon him. Everything in society depends on the law and the police being impartial and incorruptible. For example, in describing the 'founding principles' of the state of Israel, David Ben-Gurion highlights 'an independent judiciary' as 'the true safeguard of any democracy'.[12] Once these pillars of a just society are weakened, might becomes right. Everything is determined by the use of force or financial bribery.

I remember living in Indonesia back in the 1960s when corruption ruled the day. Both the police and the judiciary were fearfully corrupt, so that no one's rights were respected unless they paid a bribe. Driving tests and all other exams could be passed if one paid a bribe. Police would accuse you of dangerous driving or speeding unless you paid a bribe. Law cases were won or lost according to who paid the judge more. Corruption determined which business contracts went to whom. Actual force could also be determinative. Leading army and police officers would demand favours for themselves or their family with threats. If the favour was not granted, violence would follow. With corrupt law courts, there could be no redress for anything that was unjust or wrong. Such legal and judicial disorder spells ruin to a nation and everyone in it. And the weak and poor suffer quite particularly.

In his complaint then, no wonder Habakkuk's description of evil in Judah at that time climaxes with the fearful observation that 'the law is paralysed', 'justice never prevails', 'justice is perverted' (1:4). We may note that the prophet repeats in slightly different words his tragic observation concerning the corruption of the law. In typical Hebrew fashion this repetition underlines the importance of what is being said. And here it is even repeated *three* times; an unusually strong emphasis. Twice Habakkuk declares the awful fact of perverted justice and, added to this, he also accuses God of allowing the law to be paralysed.

Sadly, the sin of Judah all those years ago may still be witnessed today in many nations of the world. We struggle against the poverty and misery which it causes. It is right and good that we pour in developmental aid and write off national debts, but ultimately nothing will bring prosperity and peace unless the forces of the army, police and judiciary are reformed. Corruption, bribery and an unjust judiciary can still be found again and again around the world. The army and police are often the instruments of oppression rather than the forces of order and justice. Inevitably, one is moved to ask what God is doing in such situations.

Even in the old democratic nations governments constantly face the temptation to try to bring the judiciary under their power, and to use the army and police for their own political purposes. These fundamental bastions of justice and righteousness in society must maintain their independence and it is the responsibility of the whole nation to safeguard this.

'The wicked hem in the righteous'

As Habakkuk walked the streets of Judah and mingled with people in his area, he knew that the majority of people around him did not share his faith in the living God. God-fearing people were in a small minority in Judah at that time and they felt their weakness. They seemed to have so little influence and their testimony made little impact on society. Even God himself seemed impotent.

Christians today in Europe will feel a real empathy with Habakkuk and his contemporaries who followed the Lord. In Europe young people at school may well be the only Christian in their class, the teacher may stand in opposition to their faith and the curriculum may also contradict what they believe. It is not easy for teenagers to stand openly as Christians in the midst of their non-Christian classmates. And the media constantly portrays Christianity in as negative a light as possible. At home many of us live on streets where we may be the only Christians. At work we are surrounded by unbelievers. We feel that a sea of unbelief swirls around us and we seem to be like tiny sticks driven along by an irresistible current. We are swimming against the tide and we see fellow Christians' faith drowning as they give up the unequal struggle against the waves. What a relief to be reminded that God remains on his throne and that all authority has been given to him not only in heaven, but also on earth (see Mt. 28:18). But we have every sympathy with Habakkuk as he complains that 'the wicked hem in the righteous'.

'Hem in' is not necessarily a negative word, but merely reflects the fact that the wicked were surrounding the righteous. The same word occurs in Psalm 142:7 where the psalmist enjoys the prospect of the righteous gathering about him. The psalmist's prayerful hope is for this positive outworking of the Lord's goodness. In Habakkuk, however, the prophet bemoans his sad situation as he is surrounded by the wicked.

This little sentence is fitted into the context of the law being paralysed and justice being perverted. Evidently the corruption of the law was connected with the fact that the majority of people lived in iniquity. Public opinion always carries weight, even to the extent of pushing the law into making unjust decisions. This is still true today as newspaper campaigns and public opinion force politicians and the judiciary to comply with whatever is demanded of them.

Wickedness abounds in the people of God

As God's people we may be shocked when we observe the fearful godlessness and sin which so often prevail in the non-Christian society around us. And when we look out on the wider world we may despair at the corruption and evil which so obviously dominate the lives of whole societies. It may horrify us, but we are not surprised by the fact that non-Christian nations and people evidence such evil. As believers our faith is not shaken or brought into question by the evils which surround us in the lives and relationships of our non-Christian neighbours. In fact, their sin may actually confirm us in the contrasting beauty of our faith. We note the violence, broken relationships, injustices and lack of love. So we may be reassured that it is only through the resurrection life of the risen Christ, and the working of God's Holy Spirit that people can experience the inner power to enter into a life of righteousness.

But our faith may be shattered when we experience such sin within the community of God's own children. As I have myself personally experienced, it is spiritually unnerving when one is lied to by Christian leaders one has respected and trusted. As believers we expect the people of God to demonstrate holiness in their lives. We know that 'it is God's will that [we] should be sanctified' (1 Thes. 4:3) and that it is God's purpose to present his church 'without stain or wrinkle or any other blemish, but holy and blameless' (Eph. 5:27). The New Testament constantly underlines this fundamental truth that 'Christ loved the church and gave himself up for her to make her holy, cleansing her by the washing with water through the word' (Eph. 5:25–26). The Spirit of Christ is indeed the *Holy* Spirit, the one whose work it is to sanctify us from within. So it disappoints us when we find that we ourselves fail to live up to God's standards and holy expectations of us. And we are disturbed when we find all sorts of sin even in spiritual and biblical churches.

Sadly too we can study the history of God's church through the centuries and find a strange mixture of godly holiness together with terrible evils. As a Jew myself, I know that my people have not always found the Christian church innocent of violent anti-Semitism and persecuting zeal. Even Luther was guilty of hateful attitudes towards Jews and 'Turks' or Muslims. In the Reformation the solidly reformed state of Geneva with all its biblical faith and beautiful godliness also purposely drowned some Anabaptists because of their insistence on baptism by immersion.

This was the pinnacle of Habakkuk's complaint and what caused him the deep 'burden' of which he spoke in 1:1.[13] If he had merely observed idolatry and sin in the Gentile nations, he would not have been so shocked or disturbed. But the fearful catalogue of evils which he has outlined in 1:2–4 was right at the heart of Judah, God's own covenant people. One might have thought that this would shake his faith and cause him to blame God. Weaker believers might well have abandoned their faith.

Even as the covenant people of God with the reality of the indwelling Holy Spirit, we today must acknowledge that we all still have a long way to climb in the struggle towards that holiness which is God's purpose for us. Let us join Habakkuk in his sense of 'burden' because of the failures within the church of God, but let us not stumble in our faith. In recognizing our own sin and lack of holiness, let us determine to pursue godly righteousness with all our Spirit-inspired strength.

Habakkuk's response to his 'burden'

As the prophet observes Judah's tragic sin, he cries out to the Lord for help. He longs for relief from the prevailing evil and for God to renew his people with life-changing revival. Although 'call' and 'cry out' are different words, they both convey the same sense of heartfelt and almost desperate prayer. Instead of blaming God and rebelling bitterly against him Habakkuk turns to God in fervent prayer. Evidently Habakkuk's passionate intercession was not just a momentary reaction, but he persevered in his prayer of the heart. So he complains to the Lord 'how long . . . must I call for help, but you do not listen?' (1:2). We have no idea how long Habakkuk had been praying in this way, but to him it seemed an eternity.

In his use of the words 'how long' was Habakkuk feeling some identity with the psalmist's common use of these words? Rex Mason rightly points out that 'the formula "how long?" (Hebrew *'ad ānāh*) is a familiar one occurring in psalms of lament, both individual and communal, along with the synonymous *'ad māthai*.'[14] Despite their strong faith in God and trust in him, both the Psalmist and Habakkuk boldly question the working of God. As P.R. House notes

> Habakkuk represents a crucial point in the characterization of the prophet in the Twelve. Until this point all the prophets except Jonah accept the word and deeds of the Lord almost uncritically. Perhaps the prophets did not demur as long as some chance for repentance lingered, or as long as it was a foreign nation that was earmarked for destruction, but when the punishment comes to Judah, thus including the prophets themselves, questions arise. Habakkuk asks some very difficult questions.[15]

As Christians we are given a model which allows us to join the prophet in questioning what God is doing in our lives and in the world around us.

Many, even perhaps all, Christians will share at least part of the prophet's questioning, for we too have surely been through something of the same experience. We too have prayed and prayed and gone on praying for something which lies close to our hearts. Perhaps we have prayed for many years for the salvation of someone close to us. Year after year passes and we continue to cry to the Lord. But it seems as if he doesn't hear our prayer.

In Singapore there is a Chinese Buddhist temple dedicated to the sleeping Buddha. Within it there is a large statue of Buddha asleep beneath some beautiful covers. The devotees of this Buddha queue up to pray to the idol. They lift the rugs, slap the Buddha three times to wake him up and then pray. As Christians we may sometimes also be tempted to think that God is asleep. Of course, as Christians we believe the biblical promises that our Father answers prayer. We can give many lovely testimonies of specific and definite answers to prayer. That has certainly been mine and my wife's wonderful experience as a couple.[16]

But I remember listening to a conference speaker telling exciting stories of God's miraculous answers to prayer in his life. Sitting next to me was a good friend of this speaker. In the middle of the talk after one particular story my neighbour whispered to me, 'Actually, there were four years between the previous story and that one!' Did the speaker experience four years at that stage without direct answers to prayer? Again, Habakkuk's agonized 'how long, O Lord' resounds in the hearts of God's people throughout history. But Habakkuk did not give up. He still continued to cry out to the Lord, maintaining his faith that finally God would surely answer. And in that devotion to prayer (see also Col. 4:2) he also continued the same burning passion in prayer. He did not allow time to wear him down and make his prayer a cold routine.

By the end of Habakkuk 1:1–4 we wait impatiently to hear how God will answer Habakkuk's complaint and what God will do in response to his heartfelt prayer.

Two

God's Shocking Answer – I Am Using the Babylonians

Habakkuk 1:5–11

As we look back over the history of the world, we see that major changes of direction only occur very occasionally. In the last century the collapse of world empires marks just such a major new movement, with new opportunities but also new problems. In 1989 the fall of the Berlin Wall changed the course of history as the Communist empire also disintegrated, leaving America as the sole superpower.

The Bible reveals God as the arbiter of historical developments and we believe that he has his hand on everything that happens. The demise of European power in the countries of other continents spelled the beginning of considerable new growth in the church worldwide. Likewise, the collapse of Communism opened doors for the church in new ways. The courageous faith and witness of suffering Christians under Communist persecution combined with the spiritual vacuum left by the obvious bankruptcy of atheistic Marxism to make people very open to the good news of Jesus Christ. Existing churches have grown enormously and multitudes of new churches have sprung up and multiplied like mush-rooms. But problems also abound. New movements vir-tually always produce a harvest of worldly failures and inadequacies. Under the sovereign God of history new life and apparent chaos often seem to go hand-in-hand. Under such circumstances it is easy to concentrate on the negative disorder without adequately rejoicing in the growth of resurrection life.

In church history too there have been only very occa-sional times of radical change, which have left the church totally different from what it was. The New Testament reveals one such paradigm shift. The roots of Christianity were entirely Jewish – Jesus, the apostles and the first Christians were Jewish. The Bible itself was written by Jews. However, very early in the develop-ment of the church Gentiles began to flood into the con-gregations, and soon took over the leadership of the church. Jewish Christians became a tiny insignificant minority in what had been their church. This ethnic and cultural revolution has changed the whole history of the church and its essential nature theologically and in wor-ship, leadership structures and biblical understanding. European and, more recently, American forms now pre-dominate in the Christian church. Christianity's Jewish roots have been replaced. As a result, many Jewish Christians are tempted to feel that God has allowed us to be robbed of our particular forms of the Christian faith.

For several centuries now the heart of Christianity has been located in Europe and those countries to which Europeans have emigrated – North America, Australasia and South Africa. This would have surprised dignitaries in their togas in the Roman Empire during the first cen-turies of our era. But the collapse of the Roman Empire led to the massive development of Christianity in cen-tral, northern and finally Eastern Europe. And with the

Reformation and the development of Protestantism, even southern Europe joined North Africa and the Middle East in becoming the object of evangelistic missionary endeavour.

Today we are seeing another major change in the Christian church. The church's centre of gravity has shifted from north to south; from Europe to Africa, Asia and Latin America.[1] While the European churches struggle on all fronts, the churches of the south often hum with vibrant dynamism. Problems and needs abound, but their churches pulsate with confident life and growth. Inevitably, their influence within the worldwide church is growing and this will surely change the whole character of Christianity in coming years. Christians in Europe may find this difficult to comprehend and they may be quite unaware of what is happening around them. For example, in London, on an average Sunday, the ethnic British will form the minority of churchgoers. The majority will be of African, Afro-Caribbean, Korean, Chinese or other ethnic minority descent. While European Christians with blinkered vision complain of the post-Christian era, churches overseas often overflow with expectant vision – no 'post-Christian era' there!

Habakkuk too faced just such a seismic change in his day. The people of Judah were also oblivious to what was happening in the world around them. Even Habakkuk himself was in danger of looking in the wrong place for God to work. Habakkuk, and doubtless his compatriots too, were expecting God to bring new life and revival to Judah, the covenant people of God. Surely God's primary purpose was to re-establish true worship and godly holiness within Judah, God's own chosen people. But no! Habakkuk is commanded to 'look at the nations' (1:5), not at Judah. Even today, the term *goyim*, meaning 'nations', has an inherently negative implication as referring to foreign peoples who are outside the promises of God. In New Testament translation the continental Reformers even falsely translated the Greek equivalent 'the Gentiles' (*ta ethne*) as 'the heathen' (in German *die Heiden*, in French *les païens* and so on). Neither Habakkuk nor other godly people in Judah could have expected that God would be working among the despised 'nations' or Gentiles. It was reformation among their own people that they were hoping and praying for.

Might this still be the case in Britain and other countries of Europe? Many of our fervent prayers cry out for God to bring revival to our nation. Is God trying to tell us that actually he is already at work elsewhere? Instead of wallowing in self-pity as we contemplate the sin and godlessness of our nation, let us rejoice in this great truth that our God is already mightily at work.

In Acts 13:41 Paul quotes this verse from Habakkuk to warn the Jews in the synagogue in Antioch of Pisidia that they faced the same danger. If they rejected Jesus as God's means of bringing justification and the forgiveness of sins, God would turn from them to work among the Gentiles. This passage is followed immediately by Paul's history-changing announcement 'we now turn to the Gentiles' (Acts 13:46) with a supporting quotation from Isaiah 49:6 'I will also make you a light for the Gentiles, that you may bring my salvation to the ends of the earth'. So the door was now open for worldwide mission to all nations, not just to the Jews. What a surprise this must have been to those early Jewish Christians! And no wonder that unbelieving men and women hated this word from the Lord and 'stirred up persecution' (Acts 13:50). But what amazing grace that the Lord desires to bring his message of salvation and new life to all peoples everywhere! If the Gospel had been restricted only to the Jews and a few Gentile proselytes and God-fearers, the Christian faith could never have touched the British and other nations.

In Acts 13:41 Luke quotes from the Septuagint, the Greek translation of the Old Testament. This is evidently based on a different version of the Hebrew which quotes Habakkuk as saying, 'Look, you scoffers, wonder and perish, for I am going to do something in your days . . .' This version of Habakkuk fails to note the significance of the fact that God's work is to be found not in Israel as might be expected, but in the darkness of the Gentiles. But the context in which Luke uses this verse demonstrates nevertheless that he had fully appreciated the original meaning in Habakkuk. It is among the Gentiles that God is doing his work. And Luke has of course particular interest in the fact that the good news of Jesus Christ is also for Gentiles, for he was the companion of Paul, the apostle to the Gentiles[2]. Faith among the Gentiles is matched by 'scoffing' among those who rejected God's gracious working.

So God informs Habakkuk that he is already at work. The prophet had complained in 1:2–4 that God was asleep, enjoying a siesta in apparent inactivity. But God never stops working (see Jn. 5:17). Following the AV, the NIV also uses a future 'I am going to do something', but it would seem that the RSV use of the present tense is better. In either case the emphasis lies on the fact that God's working is 'in your days' (1:5). Habakkuk needed to learn that prayer for revival should not be directed towards the future, for God is already at work.

As in 1:1–4, so again here the prophet is commanded to stop blaming God. Rather he is to open his eyes to *see* God's answer to his complaint. While the Hebrew word for 'look' is just the common word for 'to see', the word translated 'watch' (Hebrew *nabat*) sounds very similar to the Hebrew word for a prophet (*nabi*). Although they are from different roots, the similarity of sound reminds us that prophets are indeed 'seers', those who live with eyes open to see what God is saying.

Although in this context the sound of the verb *nabat* may remind us of Habakkuk's prophetic call, this verb by no means always refers to such ministry. So, for example, it is also used twice of God in 1:13 – God is 'too pure to look on (*nabat*) evil' and Habakkuk asks God why he tolerates (*nabat*) evil. It is also used distinctly negatively in 2:15 where the prophet accuses the Babylonians of making people drunk so that they 'can gaze (*nabat*) on their naked bodies' – hardly a prophetic activity!

When Habakkuk begins to see what God is actually doing, he will be 'utterly amazed', an emphatic expression of total surprise. In his commentary on Habakkuk Keil calls this the 'highest degree of amazement'. Habakkuk could never have imagined that God would do such a thing. He would never have expected God to work among the Gentiles! But God's ways are not our ways and his thoughts are not our thoughts (Is. 55:8–9). He is the sovereign Lord over history. The work of his kingdom is not restricted merely to his covenant people, for he is Lord over all. He reigns in the history of the whole world. Our job is just to see what he is doing and seek to align our lives and witness to his perfect will.

The fact that God is working among the pagan Babylonians seems so incredible that God warns Habakkuk that he would not believe it even if he was told (1:5). Habakkuk's incredulity may prove more widespread. Might European Christians today also find it hard to believe what God seems to be doing? As we have seen, first-century Jewish Christians might have found it hard to believe that the church would become almost entirely Gentile. Roman and North African

Christians in the fifth century would have resisted the idea that the Roman Empire would collapse and the heart of Christianity would move north into the pagan barbarian tribes of central and northern Europe. After long centuries of sacrificial missionary work among the Huns, Goths, Visigoths and other tribes, central and northern Europe would gradually become the centre of the Christian church. In our day it is hard to picture the implications of the church's centre of gravity moving out to Africa, Asia and Latin America. What will this mean for the whole character and development of the church in the coming days? No wonder God tells Habakkuk, 'You would not believe, even if you were told'. Our questionings are based on a misunderstanding of the whole world situation.

Raising up the Babylonians

Habakkuk was amazed when God instructed him to 'look at the nations' rather than at his own people of Judah. But here is the even more outrageous statement that God was 'raising up the Babylonians' as his instruments in the outworking of his purposes. It seemed appalling that God's purposes might actually be achieved through such a terrible people. But God's ways do not always follow our ideas of what he should do. He constantly surprises, even shocks us by doing the unexpected.

God has no hesitation in describing just how awful the Babylonians were. He does not pull the wool over the prophet's eyes – the Babylonians were indeed shockingly terrible. God's description of them pulls no punches.

As David Prior vividly describes, 'God's answer to Habakkuk's lament about lawlessness and injustice is greater lawlessness and more injustice at the hands of an evil empire of terrifying cruelty'.[3] He notes that there is in 1:7 'a clear echo' of the prophet's complaint in 1:4.

But there is also a marked difference. When lamenting over Judah's evil, Habakkuk weeps over the fact that the 'Law is paralysed'. He uses the word 'Torah' for 'Law', the word of God revealed through Moses to God's covenant people. However, when describing the Babylonians' sin the Torah no longer applies. It had not been revealed to them. So Habakkuk uses the more general term *mishpat*. As Robert Culver notes, *mishpat* 'can be used to designate almost any aspect of civil or religious government'.[4] In the Old Testament it is commonly twinned with *Tsedaq*ah: righteousness. We noted with reference to 1:4 that righteousness can only flourish when the judicial system rules without corruption. Righteousness and justice embrace one another as inseparable twins.

But the Babylonians do not follow God's perfect standards of behaviour as revealed in his Law. They make up their own laws to suit their own purposes, to 'promote their own honour'. The word used for 'honour' derives from the verb 'to lift up'. The Babylonians desired to be exalted above all others. They sought their own pre-eminence and formed their laws in order to promote their own glory. So God here does not link *mishpat* to righteousness. Babylonian law focused on the Babylonians' self-centred status and had nothing to do with promoting righteousness.

In 1:6 God immediately introduces the Babylonians as 'that ruthless and impetuous people'. Devastatingly efficient and skilled, they showed no concern for others at all. In their ruthless march to power they destroyed other nations without a flicker of pity or concern. And they were 'impetuous'; in a hurry to get on with it. They brooked no delay as they swept through the world, one victory after another. Like many another arrogant nation or person they swept all opposition aside in their haste to achieve what they wanted. Patience and compassion were words which lay outside their vocabulary. Habakkuk's righteous heart is offended by the thought that the holy God could raise up such a people as his instruments.

Habakkuk 1:6 continues in its description of the Babylonians, declaring that they 'sweep across the whole earth to seize dwelling places not their own'. Like most powerful empire-builders throughout history, the Babylonians were not content with just ruling in their own area. They had greater dreams of world domination. In their pride they could never allow any other nation to rival their own universal authority. But, as we shall see later, 'the whole earth' shall finally belong to God alone, and he will vindicate his holy justice by bringing the world into 'the knowledge of the glory of the Lord' (2:14).

In their insistent march forwards, conquering area after area and people after people, the Babylonians inevitably seize places which do not belong to them. The enormity of their crimes is emphasized by the word 'dwelling-places'. There is nothing more personal than people's homes, where they live as families together. It is not without significance that the British say that 'a man's home is his castle'. But the Babylonians have no concern for such human rights or for the security and comfort of other people's lives. Their ruthless self-seeking is further underlined by the final words 'not their own'. The Hebrew has just two words which sound identical – *lō lô*, 'not his'. Ruthless ambition, whether in the international or personal sphere, shows no concern for others' welfare and the concluding *lō lô* gives the impression of

God wagging his finger at them and telling them off like naughty school children – 'Don't you dare!'

In 1:6 the word translated 'ruthless' also contains within it a sense of bitterness. In my earlier book on Habakkuk I noted that 'this word is used as a bitter cry (e.g. Gen. 27:34), of bitter water (e.g. Num. 5:18–27) or of bitterness of soul and heart (Job 3:20; Ezek. 27:31). The Chaldeans were not a happy people; bitterness filled and characterized their lives.'[5] Their amazing power and success brought them no satisfaction. Despite their abundant plunder and wealth 'they remained twisted and bitter.' In its pursuit of happiness the modern world too has much to learn from the sad example of the Babylonians. Worldly success, status and power can often coincide with an inner bitterness of spirit.

As the Babylonians drive irresistibly onwards in their conquests, their neighbours and next victims shiver in their boots. Habakkuk 1:7 declares that they are 'a feared and dreaded people'. 'Feared' and 'dreaded' are virtually synonymous, but the use of two words to describe the same characteristic underlines the terrible fear they aroused. Indeed the word 'dreaded' is often used in relationship to God himself – for example in Daniel 9:4 and Malachi 1:14. The Almighty God is so glorious and holy that without the mediation of Christ one could only tremble before him in his awesome splendour. But dread of the Babylonians is not caused by any overwhelming god-like holiness. Naked fear shivers in icy panic because of their ferocious ruthlessness.

In 1:8–10 short staccato phrases follow one after another, onomatopoeically echoing the sound of the pounding hoofs of galloping horses. As the prophet's words tumble out in rapid succession, we can almost hear the Babylonians' charges rushing from town to town. Devastation follows wherever they go. In attempting to describe this terrifying advance of the Babylonian cavalry, Habakkuk calls on his evidently intimate knowledge of wild animals. He thinks of the terrifying speed of the leopard which can outrun anything which seeks to escape. It is no use trying to run away from the Babylonians, for with their horses they will hunt down any such fugitive and destroy them. He then proceeds to describe the Babylonians in terms of a pack of hungry wolves surrounding their prey in the ominous half-light of dusk. One wolf on its own presents a formidable foe, but a whole pack hunting together is terrible. So the Babylonian army comes as one united force that nothing can withstand. Habakkuk's next image is of vultures with their sharp hooked beaks tearing the flesh away from dead or wounded bodies. One can only shudder at the thought of being torn apart by such creatures. All the time the vultures are wheeling round and round in the sky looking down to earth to see when a beast may lose the ability to resist because of sickness, injury or death. With the Babylonians on the advance it is only a matter of time before this ghastly end – and the time is short because they are so fearfully speedy in their advance. Habakkuk's final picture is the desert wind. While the translation is far from certain, the use of the desert wind[6] to describe the Babylonians' destruction of other nations calls to mind the irresistible and devastating power of a hurricane or tornado. David W. Baker notes that this picture 'is used elsewhere to symbolize devastation from the east (cf. Jer. 18:17; Hos. 12:1; 13:15) and explicitly from Babylon (Ezek. 17:10).'

We can only admire Habakkuk's rich gift of verbal expression, his use of language and in particular how his imagery is taken from the wildlife of the countryside which would have been so well-known to his audience. What a model for Christians who may be called to communicate the glory of the Gospel in today's world! His vividly pictorial teaching would fit well into the postmodern Western world of today. Jesus too loved to speak in nature parables and he used examples from everyday life and from the countryside. The Bible gives little support to dry academic theological language in preaching or teaching!

Habakkuk's picture of the vulture swooping down to devour Judah is clearly based on Deuteronomy 28:49. God's severe warning in Deuteronomy is now coming to pass. The people of God have not obeyed the Lord their God, nor observed the commands and decrees he had given them (Deut. 28:47). Therefore the judgment of God is falling upon them. Habakkuk has been complaining about God, but in reality it is God who has serious cause to blame Judah.

Both Deuteronomy and Habakkuk go on to talk of fearful sieges which culminate in the total collapse of the city walls. Nothing can protect them from God's judgment through this nation 'whose language you will not understand' (Deut. 28:49), an alien and foreign people who have no relationship to Israel and therefore no pity. In the midst of these fearful pictures of the Babylonians' horrendous advance the Lord reminds Habakkuk of his complaints about Judah. The prophet had noted the sad prevalence of 'violence' (1:2–3) in the life of God's covenant people. Now the Lord uses the same word 'violence' to describe the pagan 'hordes' of Babylon. There is evidently some similarity in their sinfulness, but the armies of Babylon surely outdo even Judah in their wickedness and callous cruelty.

Christians too may complain unhappily about weaknesses and failures within the church, but we need to be reminded of the even greater problems in non-Christian society. We ought not to take for granted the loving fellowship and spirit of service that we do experience among the people of God.

The 'desert wind' makes the prophet think of vast quantities of sand. So he continues his descriptions by saying that the hordes of Babylon 'gather prisoners like sand' (1:9). It may well have been a common expression to describe uncountable numbers. In Genesis 22:17 and 32:12 God promises Abraham and then also Jacob that their descendants would be uncountable, like the sand on the seashore. But in Habakkuk 1:9 God is not giving his people a promise, but foreseeing the victorious armies of Babylon taking 'prisoners like sand'.

Power and success can lead easily into arrogance and supercilious disregard for others. So it was to be with the Babylonians. They laugh mockingly at the leaders of other peoples who may think they are great men, but who in the eyes of the mighty Babylonians are pathetic nobodies. So it is said that the Babylonians 'deride kings and scoff at rulers'. Kings may dress up in all their finery with crowns on their heads. Rulers may sit in the places of honour and may swell with pride as they govern the lives of their people. But all their pride will fall before the advance of the invading armies.

When God determines to bring down a nation or empire, his sovereign will cannot be frustrated or stopped. What he purposes will surely come to pass. And all great kings and leaders eventually come to the end of their rule. This is true not only of political leaders, but also of the top people in business or even in the church.

The Greek translation of the Old Testament, the Septuagint, gives an insightful twist to the attitude of the Babylonians in their treatment of these kings, rulers and fortified cities. It says that the Babylonians use them like toys. They play with them and get fun from the whole game. Warfare for them is a pleasurable pastime and they enjoy it like children at play. And just as toys cannot resist rough treatment by the child, so the kings and rulers of the nations are quite unable to resist the arms of the Babylonians. The cat is playing with the mouse.

So the Babylonian armies 'laugh at all fortified cities'. They 'deride kings and scoff at rulers'. Habakkuk invites us to picture these kings and rulers with all their finery, dressed up in royal robes and seated on their thrones. Yet such outward forms of grandeur cannot conceal their weakness when the Babylonians attack. They seemed to be great men, but actually they were nothing. All leaders need from time to time to be reminded of their mortality, lest their status as presidents and prime ministers should give them a false sense of their own glory.

As Habakkuk sweeps us along with his cascading waterfall of words, impressing us with the tremendous efficiency and power of the Babylonian armies, we are suddenly shocked by 1:11 with its change in tone – 'whose own strength is their god'. With the ruthless power of military might religion seems quite irrelevant. Of course the Babylonians had their own forms of traditional religion with its particular deities and rituals, but actually it was their 'own strength' which remained at the centre of their lives. That was their god. Their guilt lay therefore not only in their ruthless cruelty and pitiless destruction of city upon city, but also in the realm of religion.

The Bible is unique in its emphasis that false worship leads inevitably to wrong living. Religion and ethics in the Bible go inseparably hand-in-hand. True worship of the living Lord will also be expressed in holy living, for we are called to be holy even as he is holy (e.g. 1 Pet. 1:15–16). This truth has particular importance for us today. With the influence from eastern religions, New Age and postmodernism have separated spirituality from ethics. Their followers can be very 'spiritual' and yet still live sadly immoral lives. In this context Christian leaders need to remember and also remind their people that moral righteousness and holiness are the essential fruit of a relationship with the holy God. In discipling new believers and in our teaching generally we need to underline God's demand that we should reflect his holiness in our daily lives and relationships.

Three

Habakkuk's Second Complaint – God, You Can't Do That!

Habakkuk 1:12–17

We cannot but feel a real sympathy with the prophet Habakkuk as he struggles to reconcile his living faith in the Lord with what God says and what he seems to be doing. In 1:2–4 Habakkuk had complained that God was ignoring the fearful sin and corruption in his people, Judah. God was just allowing his servant Habakkuk to go on seeing the violence and injustice which prevailed all around him, while not doing anything to rectify the situation.

Then in 1:5–11 God finally speaks and tells Habakkuk what he is actually doing. He is not as inactive as the prophet had thought. As so often happens with us all, God is indeed at work just when we think he is doing nothing. But his work is not at all what the prophet was expecting and hoping for. He was not bringing repentance and renewed righteousness back to Judah. He was at work among the Gentile Babylonians and raising them up as his instruments of judgment against his own covenant people. And God in his word to the prophet does not hesitate to describe the horrendous evil and barbaric cruelty of the Babylonians.

No wonder Habakkuk comes back to God with a second complaint and renewed questions. We marvel at such an open dialogue between God and the prophet. Habakkuk shares openly with God and voices his complaints at all that is happening – or not happening. And God replies with clear explanations of what his purposes are, what he is doing and what he intends to do.

As Christians we too should share with God our difficulty when we are faced with situations in our world which we cannot easily reconcile with our understanding of the nature of God. He delights in his people voicing their complaints and looking to him in faith for his answers. So in Habakkuk 1:12–17 we read Habakkuk's second complaint concerning what is happening in the world around him. He is not merely concerned for his own welfare, as is so often the case with us, but he has a wider concern for God's people as a whole and what God is or is not doing in the larger sphere of international history. This is surely a model for Christians today. We need to lift up our eyes beyond our own narrow personal interests to pray about questions of the world in which we live and the worldwide church of God of which we are a part. And our worship songs need to widen out from just the first person singular 'I' to include the wider international plural 'we'. We worship and pray to God in the context of the whole world and as members of his church worldwide.

So the fact that God is 'raising up the Babylonians' stirs up this new question: what in the world is God doing?

This fundamental question can be subdivided into four. The first problem relates to the whole question of God's eternal covenant with his people. The northern kingdom of Israel had already been conquered, exiled and scattered. If the southern kingdom of Judah is also annihilated, what does that mean? What about God's promises to Israel? Is God's covenant with Abraham and Moses to be forgotten? If God's people are eliminated by the ferocious forces of the Babylonians, then God's very word is in serious doubt. Is God truly faithful and to be trusted?

The second question also touches on the very character of God himself. If indeed he is perfect in holiness, how can he have dealings with an evil and idolatrous people like the Babylonians? Surely God in his absolute purity can only make use of pure and godly people as his instruments. And yet in 1:5–11 God has himself declared that he is raising up the Babylonians. This seems to contradict the very nature of God in his sinless perfection.

The third question relates closely to the experience of many Christians when faced with traumatic or difficult situations. So often God seems to withdraw and be silent. However much we cry to him and beg him for some explanation or word of comfort, somehow the heavens appear to be made of lead and closed against us. God remains silent. Habakkuk shares this experience of the silence of God (1:13). The prophet's only reaction is to ask the question 'why?' – the very question we are constantly advised to avoid as Christians!

The final prophetic question concludes the chapter. Will the bitter suffering under the oppression of the Babylonians never come to an end (1:17)? Is there no light at the end of the tunnel? Temporary pain and tragedy are more easily bearable when one can see the possibility of final deliverance. But when there is no hope for the future, then such interminable judgment leaves us seriously doubting God's gracious faithfulness. Can God be trusted?[1]

So Habakkuk's situation and God's word to him raise major questions concerning the nature of God himself. That is the real problem of suffering.

The background to a right response

Habakkuk's first complaint in 1:1–4 was addressed to *Yhwh*, reminding the prophet from the outset that his trust is in God himself. Likewise now in 1:12–17 Habakkuk starts his second complaint with a strong reminder of who God is. Twice he addresses his words to the Lord (1:12) with the further affirmation that *Yhwh* is 'my God, my Holy One'. In the uncertainty and anguish surrounding the nation's circumstances he then addresses God as the 'Rock', a solid foundation on which to build a deep assurance despite all that is going on around him.

Martin Luther felt that Habakkuk's heartfelt questioning of God demonstrated a weakness in his faith. However, the majority of more recent commentaries would suggest that his emphasis on the Lord reveals a deep trust in God. It is with this solid background of knowing God and trusting him that the prophet can open his heart to the Lord. All the evidence seems to contradict his faith in God, but he clings on nevertheless. Knowing that God is his only 'rock', he can afford to voice his complaints and present his questionings to the Lord. So the character of the God he trusts is the background to his honest openness. His complaints are not merely internal grumblings in his own thoughts; they are addressed to God. If grumbling is not turned into prayer to the living God, it can easily lead to bitterness. So Habakkuk sets us a good example in a context where there seems to be no end to our difficulties and God seems to be silent and inactive. An affirmation of the nature of God should form the background to a right response.

We notice that Habakkuk is assailed by opposing voices. On the one hand he cannot understand what God is doing. But at the same time, he firmly bases his complaints in the context of an unquestioning assurance of the nature of God as perfectly holy and just. In this he is very typically human. Christians too live with that same combination of faith and doubt, rejoicing and complaining. We note this same pattern in Matthew 28 where the two women worshipped the resurrected Jesus while being 'afraid yet filled with joy' (Mt. 28:8). Likewise, the apostles worshipped him 'but some doubted' (Mt. 28:17). It was these same worshipping and doubting disciples who were then sent out to make disciples of all nations. Like the prophet Habakkuk we may indeed question God, but our doubts need to be bracketed with a deep inner assurance of God.

'Lord'

In his Tyndale Old Testament commentary David W. Baker states that 'not only God's eternity but also his active involvement in Israel's history is shown by the use of his covenant name Yhwh (cf. Ex. 6:2–8).' In a context where God seems to be inactive and powerless it is good to lay down the marker right at the outset that God is the covenant Lord of history. And to underline his emphasis on 'the Lord', Habakkuk repeats the title twice in 1:12. In my previous book on Habakkuk I wrote

> This very personal title 'Jehovah' or 'Yahweh' was revealed to Moses in Exodus 3 and underlines the intimate personal nature of the living God. He is not just the philosophical ground of our being. He is no remote deity. He is the Lord Jehovah, who is intensely personal. He feels, he wills, he loves, he plans, he hates, he blesses and judges. The Lord is active in accordance with his personal character and nature.

Again and again in the Bible we are presented with cat-
alogues of one past event after another in the history of
Israel, showing how God has been active as sovereign in
leading his people. Throughout history he has not only
judged them when they turned against him in idolatry
and sin, but he has also wonderfully saved them and
blessed them. *Yhwh* may seem to be asleep while catas-
trophe falls on his people, but actually he is always
working out his purposes of grace. As we have already
seen, he may sometimes work in unexpected ways and
not always in accordance with what we might desire. But
what he does is perfect and ultimately it becomes clear
that his ways are indeed higher than ours. Remembering
what God has done both for us personally and for his
people throughout history gives us reassurance when
we doubt and question God.

So it is sometimes good to look back over the centuries
of history and see how God has led his church and
worked on behalf of his people. It is good to recall all
that God has done in saving and blessing us individually and as a family. God has perfect purposes both for
his covenant people from generation to generation in
history and also for each one of his children very personally. The old children's chorus used to exhort us to
'count your blessings, name them one by one'. As children of God we can look back and see the hand of God
weaving the tapestry of our lives. The memory of the
past can give us a firm foundation as we face the sufferings and uncertainties of today.

The name *Yhwh* reminds the prophet also of God's
covenant with his people. He has made definite promises to us and surely God will never break his word. His
promises are sure. Habakkuk can rest his head in confidence on the pillow of the Lord's covenant promises.
However badly they may suffer now under the

judgment of God, ultimately Judah may be assured that God will never totally destroy his people. Sin and rebellion against God bring upon them the heavy hand of divine displeasure, but the covenant promises will remain constant. As Christians we are reminded that the covenant with Israel leads to the coming of the Messiah Jesus, who fulfils to perfection all the will of God for humanity and for Israel. He is the second Adam, the perfect human being. Likewise he is the unique seed of Abraham, the father of Israel (Gal. 3:16) and 'of many nations' (Rom. 4:17). He is also the perfect seed of David, the great King of Israel (Rom. 1:3). Finally and completely the promises of God to his people find their fullness in the coming of Jesus Christ. So Jesus reveals himself in John's Gospel as the great 'I am', *Yhwh* now present with his people in saving glory and power.

'My God'

Having addressed his prayer to the Lord, Habakkuk now further addresses 'My God' using the Hebrew *Elohim*. In the creation story in Genesis 1 and 2 the creator is called *Elohim*. In Genesis 2 *Elohim* is linked directly with *Yhwh*, 'the Lord God'. Like the English 'God', the word *Elohim* reminds us therefore of the creative power of God. He is high above in majesty and splendour, but he also acts creatively in the world. In many tribal religions the high creator deity lives in splendid isolation from the world, too glorious to relate to mere humans or to the created order. Similarly, the former tribal religion of the Arabs before Mohammed still has an influence within Islam. So Muslims find that the creator Allah is so high and great that intimate personal relationship with him becomes impossible. In eastern religions the whole idea of a beneficent creator has been largely lost.

But the Bible underlines not only the distant glory and transcendence of the creator God, but also his relationship to us as human beings and to all creation. So it is that Habakkuk calls him *'my* God', stressing the reality of God's very personal relationship with him.

While the early chapters of Genesis use the word *Elohim* for the creator, later books of the Old Testament also use other names. In Genesis 14 the heathen Melchizedek introduces *El* into the biblical narrative. *El* was the high creator deity worshipped by all the heathen nations around Israel in the Middle East, so the non-Hebrew Melchizedek would naturally have believed in *El*. After Genesis 14 the creator is still often referred to as *Elohim*, but now also as *El*. So the heathen creator deity is adopted into the religious life of God's people, but his nature and character are adapted from their heathen background and fitted into the biblical revelation. So *Elohim* and *El* become interchangeable names. Later Israel is banished in exile to Babylon and there comes in contact with the Babylonian high creator deity who was called *Elah*. *Elah* is then also adopted into biblical faith and adapted in the understanding of his character and ways of working. The biblical books of Ezra and Daniel use *Elah* freely for *Elohim*, while Jeremiah also uses this name once (10:11). No other Old Testament book calls the creator *Elah*.[2]

When the Christian faith began to spread in Europe, the local tribal religions worshipped such high creator deities as 'God' in Britain, *'Dieu'* in France and *'Bog'* in Russia. Again the first European Christians had no hesitation in adopting and adapting these heathen titles for the Creator, although they rejected utterly all idol deities. While these idols' names still linger on, for example in the names of the days of the week (Woden's day, Thor's day and so on), like the Baalim before them they were totally banished from every expression of the Christian faith.

The Bible's adoption of the high creator deity of other peoples has of course considerable significance in the practice of Christian mission among other faiths today. Likewise, the complete rejection of the lower level shrine deities like the Baalim should also present us with a model as we bring the gospel of Jesus Christ to other cultures and peoples.

Habakkuk does not here in 1:12 refer to *El*, let alone to the Babylonian *Elah* who he would not yet have encountered. His mind and heart go back to the biblical story of the creation. His cry goes up to *Elohim*, the glorious creator of all the world. In traditional Jewish thought the story of creation reminds us that God is Lord over *all* the world and *all* peoples. He is not just the God of Israel, but of *all* (e.g. 2 Kgs. 19:15; Ps. 24:1–2). As the creator God he is therefore sovereign over the Babylonians as well as over Judah. What a comforting reassurance for the prophet as he contemplates the advance of the brutal armies of the Babylonians! And what a comfort too for us in our day as we observe the overwhelming influence of ungodly people and philosophies! We may sometimes feel impotent in the face of the non-Christian world around us, but we are reminded that even in international affairs God remains in control. And in the advance of pluralism, with its intolerance towards people of faith, our God still has authority on earth as well as in heaven. We are therefore ready to stand firm against all opposition, whatever the persecution and suffering which may come upon us. The great truths associated with the expression 'my God' may lift us from despondency to praise.

'My Holy One'

The basis of Habakkuk's problem lies in his assurance that God remains absolutely holy in his essential nature.

It is because of the nature of God that the problem of suffering and evil is so acute. How can God tolerate the triumph of such diabolical forces as the Babylonians? How can he possibly allow them to devastate so many nations, let alone claim that he has himself raised them up as his agents in the whole development of history?

Some religions which lack this emphasis on God's complete holiness face the problem of evil and suffering without undue heart-searching. They merely assert that God is all-powerful and he can do what he wants. Other faiths believe particularly in the doctrine of *Karma*, the law of cause and effect. So if there is suffering, or if evil prevails, it must be due to the sin of those at the receiving end. This sin may have been committed in the present life or it may be from a previous incarnation. Tragedy is therefore not something which elicits sympathy or compassionate help, but a shrug of the shoulders because 'it serves them right'; they deserve all they are getting.

Habakkuk faces the problem squarely. As the Bible constantly reminds us, God is the 'Holy One'. He is always and at all times completely faultless in his burning purity and total trustworthiness. There can be no shadow of anything less than ideal in God. Total moral holiness characterizes everything he is and everything he does. As the Bible tells us, he cannot lie (Tit. 1:2; Heb. 6:18). He is consistently just in all his doings and judgments (Rom. 3:26). And biblical concordances present us with long lists of verses asserting the holiness of God. No other religion gives the holiness of God such absolute prominence, but biblical faith is built on this foundation. But this great truth has to be squared with what is actually happening. How can such a holy God contemplate sinful people like the Babylonians and continue to tolerate their victorious march as they trample down nation after nation?

Wonderfully, the Hebrew suffix meaning 'my' is added both to the word 'God' and to the further assertion that God is the 'Holy One' – '*My* God, *my* Holy One'. It is not only the sovereign God in all his supreme creative power and glory that is in an intimate personal relationship with his people. As his people we are also allowed to have that same close personal relationship with God in all his dazzling holiness. Yet how can this be, when the Bible also asserts that nobody can see God and live, for he is 'the invisible God' (Col. 1:15)? Gloriously, Paul declares in Colossians 1 that in Jesus Christ we have 'the image' of that invisible God, so that the invisible becomes visible and the unknowable becomes knowable. Through our relationship with Jesus the unapproachably holy God has become '*my* Holy One'. And, centuries before the coming of Christ, the prophet Habakkuk was enjoying this reality. The fruit of Jesus' reconciling work stretches back into Israel's history as well as forwards into the life of the Christian church. Immanuel, God with us, was a present reality even before its perfect climax in the coming of Jesus Christ into this world.

'*Rock*'

With the coming onslaught of the Babylonians Habakkuk's world was throbbing with uncertainty. No one could imagine what the future might hold. Fear and anxiety stalked the streets and homes of Jerusalem. Rebellion against God prevailed throughout the people. It is in this context that Habakkuk looks to God as his 'Rock', the one and only sure and stable reality he could cling to. Against all odds, it was on this Rock as the one solid foundation that he could build his life and faith.

In our contemporary world we also face real uncertainties. Nothing is stable in our constantly changing societies. Everything comes and goes with eye-blinking rapidity – fashions, music, manners, vocabulary. Nothing lasts, even marriage and jobs. What an insecure world we live in! But God remains our secure Rock in the midst of this insecurity and anxiety. As Keil says in his old commentary on Habakkuk, the prophet finds his peace in this 'unchangeable refuge'. And Habakkuk is not alone in this. Moses also trusted God as his Rock (Deut. 32:4,15,18,30–31). David too in the midst of his trials rejoices in God as his Rock (Ps. 28:1; 31:2; 61:2; 62:2,6–7 and so on). So Jesus encourages us to lay the foundation of our lives on the solid Rock (Mt. 7:24; Lk. 6:48). When our faith is built on God as our Rock, the storms may rage – but the house will stand.

So Habakkuk's second complaint in 1:12–17 begins with his assured reminder that in the midst of every traumatic suffering at the hands of the Babylonians God is still the Lord, 'my God, my Holy One', the Rock. Only after this almost creedal affirmation can the prophet proceed to voice his questionings in prayer.

1:12: Judgment, but we will not die

In 1:4 the prophet had seen the tragedy of a corrupted justice system in Judah. He had complained to the Lord that 'justice never prevails' and indeed 'is perverted'. God's desire is that justice (Hebrew *mishpat*) should rule as the foundation for society in the life of his people Israel. In earlier years God had established judges (in Hebrew 'judges' has the same root as *mishpat*) to lead Israel with justice. But sadly his purposes had been frustrated and Israel had rebelled against God's ways. As so often in this world, rebellion against God led to an increasing misuse of the whole legal system and therefore the true law (Torah, the law of God) deteriorated into injustice.

Now the same word 'justice' comes again in 1:12 (NIV 'judgment'). The Lord is indeed just and can be trusted to execute perfect justice, but sadly sometimes his justice is more of a threat than a promise to the people of God. Habakkuk had thought that God was inactive and therefore injustice ruled in Judah, but actually God was at work executing justice through the Babylonians. But now that justice of God comes to destroy and to judge, rather than to bring *Shalom* and the blessings of God. As the NIV translation indicates therefore, God's justice can now be equated with 'judgment'.

We may observe from this verse that God's divine 'justice/judgment' is by no means haphazard. It is no accident of history that the Babylonians are sweeping through the nations, bringing fearful suffering and tragedy. Habakkuk may object, but God has 'appointed' them as his means of justice. Habakkuk here uses a strong word which carries the idea of firmly establishing something or purposefully placing something in position. Likewise, the Hebrew for 'ordained' is used for the laying of a firm foundation. It is used, for example, for Solomon as he begins to build the great Temple in Jerusalem.

How good it is to be reminded that the triumphant march of evil nations is under the firm control of the God of all justice. His purposes of justice will prevail – even if it means that God vindicates his holiness through judging and punishing his people for their sinful rebellion against him. The very strength of the word 'appointed' forces Habakkuk to be aware that his objections have no hope of overruling the fixed purpose of almighty God.

In our morally slack Western world today the idea of God punishing people and exercising holy justice in judgment seems unacceptable. But Habakkuk's faith is based on the biblical truth that our God is the 'Holy One'.

Happily, the judgment of God has its limits. It will not last for ever. God's covenant promises remain intact and he will keep his word despite the sin of his people. With that confidence Habakkuk affirms 'we will not die'. Ultimately God's love for Israel will break through the dark cloud of judgment and bring the sunshine of his grace. What a comfort to us all!

As with everything else in Habakkuk's life of discipleship, this assurance of God's final grace and blessing in accordance with his covenant promises is based on his understanding of the nature of God himself. God is 'from everlasting', so surely we as his followers must also have an eternal future. The congregation of Israel will widen out into God's international church with Jew and Gentile together in the glorious international purposes of God. And his church shall abide eternally, the very 'gates of hell will not overcome it' (Mt. 16:18). So we may observe that with God there is a definite strength of purpose both in his ordaining the Babylonians as his means of punishment and in his everlasting covenant so that 'we will not die'. His promises are sure and we rest our heads on this pillow. Any complaints? Absolutely not!

1:13: God's absolute purity

In the past this verse has been widely used in evangelism to explain the human predicament. In his absolute burning purity and holiness God can have nothing to do with anything even slightly corrupted. He cannot contemplate evil. The holiness of God can have nothing in common with sin. So Christians would explain to their non-Christian friends that our sin separates us from God. No wonder that so many people share the same experience of trying to pray and feeling that their prayers seem to hit the ceiling and bounce back to them unheard. They find that God seems distant and impossible to reach. Famously, a well-known Russian cosmonaut was said to have declared that even in outer space he had not encountered God! Sin forms an impenetrable barrier between God and the person whose sin remains uncleansed.

Then the Christian witness would rightly elaborate on the glorious truth that Jesus Christ has taken the burden of our sin upon himself on the cross. He has paid the penalty for all our corruption and evil. That is why when dying on the cross he cried out 'My God, my God, why have you forsaken me?' (Mt. 27:46; Mk. 15:34). He took all our sin and its penalty upon himself, thus opening the door for us to be cleansed from all that is evil or imperfect in us. As we become followers of Jesus, he totally releases us from all that previously separated us from the holy God.

But when Habakkuk declares that God is too pure even to look on evil and that he cannot 'tolerate wrong', he is not just thinking of God's reaction to our sin as individuals. He is particularly aware of the corporate sin of the Babylonian hordes. In its Greek translation of the Old Testament the Septuagint here changes the original Hebrew. In Hebrew 'evil' refers to human beings, but in the Septuagint 'evil' is in the neuter case and so means 'evil things'. But the prophet is thinking very definitely of the impossibility of God relating to human beings. How can the holy God even contemplate the possibility of using such desperately evil people as his instrument? How can God remain silent when the Babylonians 'swallow up' the whole people of Judah?

The expression 'swallow up' must have conjured up powerful images in Habakkuk's mind and in those who heard his message. It would have reminded them of how the earth had 'swallowed' (Ex. 15:12) the Egyptian army as it pursued the Israelites fleeing from captivity in Egypt. As the Egyptians followed the Israelites across the Red Sea, God 'blew with [his] breath and the sea covered them. They sank like lead in the mighty waters' (Ex. 15:10–12). In Numbers 16:30–34 the word 'swallow up' is repeated several times of God causing the earth to swallow up evil people like Korah, and the cry goes up from Israel that 'the earth is going to swallow us too!'. Jeremiah would also use the same expression to describe Judah's destruction at the hands of the Babylonians: 'Like a serpent he has swallowed us and filled his stomach with our delicacies, and then has spewed us out.' (Jer. 51:34). In Jeremiah 51:44 the prophet again uses the same picture of Babylon spewing out what he has swallowed. And the prophet Jonah soon learned that disobedience to God and refusal to preach to the Gentiles in Nineveh led to him being swallowed up by a large fish.

In 1:1–4 Habakkuk was deeply troubled and 'burdened' by the violence and wrongdoing of Judah, the people of God. But now in his mind he finds that Judah is comparatively 'righteous' when put alongside the Babylonians, although he uses the same word 'wicked' to describe both Judah and the Babylonians. But in general Babylonian violence makes Judah look like a gentle lamb.

1:14–16: Babylonian fishing

While Judah is compared to chaotic 'sea creatures that have no ruler' (1:14), the Babylonians are referred to in

the singular as one united army. They act as one in disciplined and frightening power. In contrast Judah is
described by Davidson in his commentary as 'a mere
swarming disorder' like some lower forms of life which
'have no higher instincts, no organization'.

As Christians too we need to learn that chaotic disunity militates against our effectiveness as witnesses for
Christ, while a loving and disciplined unity will make it
easier for people to see the reality of our faith. As Jesus
himself declared in John 13:35, 'All men will know that
you are my disciples, if you love one another'. We need
to repent of our sinful disunity and our self-glorifying
empire-building in our evangelistic mission, seeking
only to extend our own denomination or form of
Christian church. As we have already noted, the model
of God in Trinity challenges us to serve one another in
humble unity.

Habakkuk's picture of fishermen pulling up their
catch of fish with hooks (see also Amos 4:2) relates to the
Assyrian practice of leading their captives away by ropes
fastened to hooks in the under-lip. The prophet then
vividly describes how the victorious Babylonians treat
their captives by the parallel of 'he catches them in his
net' and 'he gathers them up in his dragnet'. As O.
Palmer Robertson explains in his commentary on
Habakkuk, contemporary inscriptions depict the
Babylonian gods dragging 'a net in which their captured
enemies squirm'.

The frightening cruelty of the Babylonian military is
further heightened by their 'fiendish gloating' as they
rejoice and are glad (1:15). The Babylonians' gloating
reminds us of how they laughed at all fortified cities
(1:10) and played with kings and rulers as if they were
children's toys. And while they sadistically enjoy the
sight of other peoples' fearful suffering, they themselves

'live in luxury and enjoy the choicest food'. At the same time as they are inflicting desperately cruel degradation on their captives, they are relaxing in luxury and feasting sumptuously. With such a fearful picture in mind it is no wonder that Habakkuk has some hard questions to place before God.

In modern times the idea of 'luxury' has become something negative and unjust. But in the Old Testament the word is normally only used positively. For example, it describes the fatness of milk and honey in the Promised Land of Canaan and plentiful prosperity in Egypt (e.g. Gen. 41:2). Thus Habakkuk implies that the Babylonians are enjoying at Judah's expense the good life which Israel was promised if they would but follow the Lord in holy obedience. Perhaps it also underlines the fact that Judah's humiliation comes as God's righteous judgment. God has so ordained things that sin always has dire consequences. The people of God were tragically missing out on the delights which God longed to impart to them.

In his commentary David Baker points out concerning the words 'sacrifice' and 'burn incense' that 'each time the two verbs are used together, it is invariably involving pagan worship in almost a fixed formula of condemnation'. Following the usual biblical emphasis, false worship is here linked inseparably with evil behaviour. Worship and ethics must go hand-in-hand together because our God is perfect in holiness. We have already observed the same truth in 1:11 where again the Babylonians' cruelty is linked to their idolatry.

1:17: How long, O Lord?

The brutal cruelty of 1:15 and the idolatrous and gloating luxury of 1:16 lead on to Habakkuk asking the vital question of 1:17. Will the Babylonians go on destroying nations for ever? Will God never bring peace? Will he not at some stage vindicate his righteous justice and bring an end to the Babylonians' triumphant march?

This question is an exact parallel with the same questions Habakkuk had raised in the very first verses of the book. His first complaint had begun with the same question: 'how long, O Lord . . .?' (1:2). Now he has affirmed that God himself is 'from everlasting' (1:12) with the implication that his covenant promises can never be broken, but abide from generation unto generation. But the ongoing continual triumph of these idolatrous Babylonians would seem to contradict Habakkuk's fundamental faith. So his question reflects not only his longing for relief from the horror of Judah's degradation at the hands of these Babylonians. He is also longing for God to demonstrate that his faith is true and that God is indeed trustworthy in his justice and holiness.

The psalmist had affirmed that 'the Lord reigns for ever' and that he 'will judge the world in righteousness; he will govern the peoples with justice' (Ps. 9:8). Habakkuk is crying out to God to bring these truths to pass in reality. It is not always easy to reconcile the vicious violence of evil and ungodly people or nations with the assertion that God is the sovereign Lord of history and the just judge over all. Such faith statements seem almost naïve in the light of what we see and hear on television and in the newspapers.

So Habakkuk's problems mount up. How can God remain silent when he sees the fearful wrongdoing of his own covenant people? Why does he remain silent when the prophet cries to him in fervent prayer, day after day and month after month? Then Habakkuk has difficulty with God's answer. How can the holy God raise up such arrogant and merciless people as the Babylonians to bring judgment on Judah for their rebellion? Perhaps the prophet might have found it acceptable that God had to judge the sin of his people, but surely not through such unholy people. What has happened to God's absolute unapproachable holiness? And what about his covenant and promises which should abide for ever? So must the judgment be without end? Torment is just about acceptable and bearable if we can see an end to it. But is there no light at the end of the tunnel? Will the Babylonian horde 'keep on emptying his net' and 'destroying nations without mercy?'

Today too as we listen to the news and read our newspapers, we may also wonder what the God of history is doing. Is he really sovereign over all? Can we still trust him as the supreme God over history? And is he really directing our personal lives according to his loving purposes of grace? It is with such questions in mind that I have called my life story *Life's Tapestry*, because as Christians we believe that the bafflingly incomprehensible strands of life are being woven step by step into a beautiful and meaningful picture. Our God's righteousness and justice will be vindicated. We cry out to him and await his answer.

Four

How Will God Answer? – Though It Seem Slow, Wait for It!

Habakkuk 2:1–4

When Habakkuk openly complains to the Lord and makes clear his concerns, the Lord gives him a direct answer. So it was in Habakkuk chapter one. In 1:1–4 the prophet declared his deep concern at the rampant evil in Judah. God then reassured the prophet that he was already at work, although he seemed to Habakkuk to be asleep and inactive. He was raising up the Babylonians. That led to Habakkuk's second complaint which we have just seen in 1:12–17. Habakkuk's heart and mind were full of objections and faith-shaking questions, but still in the midst of it all he clung on to the Lord as 'my God, my Holy One' and as his Rock of refuge.

In 2:1 we shall observe the seer's response to his own questions and complaints. Then we shall hear the beginnings of God's final answer which will occupy the rest of Habakkuk chapter two.

2:1: Habakkuk's response to his difficulties

All of us, from time to time, face situations which are beyond our ability to understand. We cannot make sense of what is happening to us or all around us. Everything seems to contradict what we believe concerning God. Our whole faith is challenged and we feel we could easily sink into the mire of unbelief. Is God still faithful? And how shall we react to our problems?

Habakkuk is determined to get an adequate answer from the Lord and takes all the necessary steps to make sure he does. But today we so easily surrender weakly and allow our troubles to undermine our faith and wreck our lives. We could do well to take a leaf out of Habakkuk's book and seek a word from the Lord with all our energy.

In describing his determination to see what God has to declare to him, the prophet uses vivid imagery. He will be like a keeper of the watch (see 2 Kgs. 11:5–7; 2 Chr. 23:6; Neh. 7:3). He stations himself on the ramparts of the city walls so that he can easily see anyone approaching the city. No enemy will be able to sneak up unobserved to attack and destroy. The prophet has his eyes open to see what God will do and indeed is already doing.

It has been suggested that Habakkuk may actually be using a different image, not that of a guard on the ramparts of the city walls. It is possible, but a little unlikely, that Habakkuk saw himself standing on a watch-tower in the middle of a field of ripe crops, watching for birds coming to eat the corn.

In either case it is clear that the prophet is keeping a close watch on events and is determined to see God's answer to the complaints he has so boldly declared to the Lord. This disciplined determination is evidenced by the fact that he will 'stand' to watch. He will not sit or lie down lest he fail to note what is going on. A soldier on guard or anyone watching over the crops against hungry birds must never relax in a sitting or lying position. So he 'stations himself' on the ramparts, using the word which is also used for a sadly determined life of evil in Ps. 36:4 – 'he commits himself to a sinful course'. In 2 Chronicles 20:17 King Jehoshaphat and the people of Jerusalem are commanded to *'take up your positions*; stand firm and see the deliverance the Lord will give you'.

As Christians too we need not only to wait for God to give us his word in response to our prayers, but actively to place ourselves in a position to hear and see his purposes.

Again, as in the first verses of this book, it is with open eyes that the prophet expects to *see* God's word. Seeing has priority over just hearing. While the NIV has the prophet saying 'I will *look* to see . . .' the old Authorised or King James Version more accurately uses an active word of careful observation 'and will *watch* to see'.

The word 'watch' reminds us of Jesus' word to his disciples in the Garden of Gethsemane as he faces the agony of his impending crucifixion. The disciples had endured a heavy week. It had been exceedingly busy and tiring, but also emotionally draining. Any sensible doctor or counsellor would have advised them that they would benefit from a good relaxing sleep. It was therefore too demanding just to tell them to pray with Jesus. A straight order to pray would have been asking the impossible. So Jesus requests them to *'watch* and pray' lest they fall into temptation. They desperately needed to take a disciplined stand and carefully watch. Only then might they be able to withstand sleep and actually pray. Sadly, we know what happened. They failed to watch carefully and sleep overtook them. In his time of trial Jesus stood alone without his disciples' fellowship and support in prayer. He had warned them that failure to watch and pray would lead to them falling into temptation. In fact the consequences of those three disciples' failure to watch and pray affected the whole body of the disciples, for in Jesus' final hour of need at the crucifixion itself they all 'deserted him and fled' (Mt. 26:56). Three men failed to watch and pray, and the whole body of disciples deserted the Lord. Is this still true today? When some of us fail to pray like those three disciples in the Garden of Gethsemane, is that the background cause of weakness and failure in God's church?

It is evident that Habakkuk fully expected God to speak to him as he carefully scrutinized all that was going on around him and in world events. He was not just voicing his complaints, but at the same time expecting God to reveal his answers. He seems to have desired that God would in this way give him his directions through his own thoughts and understanding. So just how was he imagining God's word coming?

Although the NIV translates 2:1 so that Habakkuk was looking to see what God would say *to* him, the Hebrew could perhaps more accurately be translated as '*in* me'. So God's word is not coming to Habakkuk just from outside through the events of contemporary history, but particularly it comes from within the prophet's own thoughts as he contemplated and prayed. We may be reminded of Paul's amazingly confident assertion that 'we have the mind of Christ' (1 Cor. 2:16). Does Habakkuk have that same assurance that his thoughts are wonderfully attuned to the very thoughts of God himself? Is he asking God to direct his thinking, so that he may know within himself what God has determined?

As Christians we also long that God would make us increasingly like himself in our thoughts, dreams and ambitions. As we pray, we want God to mould our thinking so that we also have God's answers within ourselves. We want to steep ourselves in Scripture so that we too might increasingly have the mind of Christ and thus know 'what he will say *in* me'.

Like Habakkuk we may then also know what answer we should give if we have particular difficulties and complaints. It may be right for us boldly to voice our complaints to the Lord, but only if we determine to find God's answers as we bring ourselves into line with God's will and purposes. This will require determined prayer and study of the Bible as his word to us. It will also mean that we should keep our eyes open to see what God is doing in our own lives, in the church and around us in the world.

Commentaries and Bible translations in their footnotes rightly point out that this verse could possibly be translated as 'what to answer when I am rebuked', although this translation carries less weight than the standard versions of this verse. But of course all of us will face times when we have to suffer other peoples' criticisms and rebukes. We may blame God, but then we in our turn are attacked by other people. Those of us who have public ministries, as did the prophet Habakkuk, will inevitably find ourselves and our ministries criticized from time to time. This may prove particularly difficult to handle if we are somewhat insecure within ourselves and lack a true self-confidence. But all of us in such circumstances need to gain our personal sense of self-worth through a deep realization that God loves and esteems us. True self-confidence rests on what God thinks of us rather than the opinions of other people.

True though this may be, it does not seem appropriate to the context of what Habakkuk is saying. While noting this possible translation, we therefore return to the idea

that Habakkuk was carefully looking out to see what
answer he would himself give to his own complaint. He
complains and he himself will give the answer.

2:2–4: The Lord begins his answer

While the NIV follows Habakkuk's determination to dis-
cover God's response to his complaint with the words
'Then the Lord replied', the Hebrew in no way implies a
time sequence. It is not saying that the prophet stood at
his watch and stationed himself on the ramparts and
then the Lord replied. But there is a definite connection
between 2:1 and 2:2. The latter verse starts with 'and',
introducing the reality that Habakkuk's attitude and
God's answer belong together. When we are determined
to find God's mind and purposes, he does reveal his will
to us. Our earnest desire and his word to us belong
inseparably together.

God was determined that his revelation to Habakkuk
should be absolutely and unmistakably clear. There was
to be no uncertainty about what God had determined for
the history of his people and likewise that of the
Babylonians. The people of Judah in general and
Habakkuk in particular should be left in no doubt as to
what God was planning.

So Habakkuk is commanded to 'write down the revelation'. Spoken words may be forgotten or even falsified,
but what is written cannot be denied. When God's purposes are fulfilled and actually come to pass, they can be
checked against the revealed prophecies in their written
form. In this way it may be guaranteed that people will
know that God has worked. The events of history are not
just chance. God works out his purposes and his
prophetic will is fulfilled.

These words remind us that it is often helpful to write down what we feel God has said to us in our devotional times with him. Then later we can look back and see how he has kept his word and we can have renewed assurance as we praise him.

God goes on to tell Habakkuk to 'make it plain on tablets, so that a herald may run with it'. An alternative reading suggests that it is not 'a herald' who runs, but rather the one who reads the written revelation from the Lord. In either case God's word is to be so clearly written that it is totally 'plain' to the reader.

There are two possible interpretations of the final phrase of this verse, but both convey the same basic sense. It may be that God is saying that the revelation is to be written so that its meaning is so clear that a herald will run to declare it to the people. He will have no doubts concerning the message and its urgency, so he will not dawdle. He will *run* to declare God's word to all who will listen. The clarity of God's word carries with it a burning urgency.

The other possible interpretation emphasizes that God's word is to be so legibly written on the tablets that the herald or other reader may actually be able to read it while running. What a delightfully humorous picture! Despite the tablets bobbing up and down while the herald runs, he may nevertheless be able to read the words clearly while still running. This not only underlines the clarity of the message, but also the urgency. The herald or runner will not need to pause from his running in order to read and thus waste time. He can continue running at full speed and still the writing will be plain enough for him to read it at the same time.

So God's message is to be clear and urgent in its vital importance. But it is also an assured word. It 'will not prove false', 'it will certainly come'. Against the background of our human impatience it may seem terribly slow, for we are tempted always to long for God to act on our behalf *now*, not just at some stage in the apparently indefinite future. Modern humanity is even more impatient than previous generations. We have today little sense of the future and desire everything to happen in the present, today and not tomorrow.

But God's 'revelation awaits an appointed time' and it will certainly come to pass at that God-determined time. So God declares reassuringly to the prophet that in God's perfect timing 'it will not delay'. What God has foretold will take place at exactly the time which God has planned for it.

God therefore says to Habakkuk, 'though it linger, wait for it'. The RSV has the pertinent translation, 'though it seem slow, wait for it'. And it often does – God frequently seems fearfully slow to act. The Japanese theologian Kosuke Koyama called one of his books *Three Mile an Hour God*. He says that God does not travel by jet plane, but crawls slowly along by water buffalo cart. God does not rush. We may blame God for being so slow to act, but our criticisms will not change his mind. He knows what is best.

If we had been in God's place, the Messiah would probably have come several centuries earlier! Would we have waited for century after century? As modern people we find it hard to conceive of the possibility of God waiting patiently in four hundred years of divine silence between the time of Malachi, the final Old Testament prophet, and the coming of John the Baptist. But God knew the need for careful preparation of his people and of the circumstances of history before he could send Jesus to live, die and be raised again. If Jesus had come some centuries earlier, his coming would doubtless have been a failure. Whatever we may feel,

God has infinite patience and is willing to wait for exactly the right time.

So it is now for Habakkuk. As we have noted in 1:2–4 God seems to be asleep and inactive. Habakkuk watches the implacable advance of the Babylonians and foresees the inevitable defeat of God's people. They will be taken away into captivity and exile with horrendous cruelty. He must have wondered where it was all leading. Did God still have a final purpose and, if so, when would it come to pass?

In that context God instructs the prophet to write down the vision of God's revealed purposes so that no one can forget it. It must be so clear that they will remember it when it does finally eventuate. Habakkuk is told to press on with patience even though God seems so slow to fulfil his word of promise.

In the rush of modern life and the spiritual impatience of so many of us, perhaps this command should become our watchword. 'Though it linger, wait for it.' We would do well to have it posted on our bulletin board or written in large letters next to our bed or on our desk. God's revelation *will certainly come and will not delay.*

In 2:4 godly patience is contrasted with being 'puffed up' and is described as being 'righteous'. The description of the Babylonians as 'puffed up' contains the sense of presumptuous pride – the same basic picture as the British expression 'big head'. The same word is used in Numbers 14:41,44 where Israel insisted on 'disobeying the Lord's command' (Num. 14:41) and went ahead of Moses and the ark of the Lord's covenant. Perhaps Habakkuk would have recalled the use of this word in Numbers 14 with the warning that such presumption led inexorably to utter defeat. Would the Babylonians in their pride also be routed in days to come? Certainly they exhibited the same presumptuous pride, advancing in battle without consideration of the will of God.

And, as it always does, that pride led inexorably to moral failure. When people have an inflated sense of their own absolute competence and ability, they soon develop a lifestyle which is 'not upright'. Conceited pride and moral failure belong together. This fundamental principle proves true in every generation and in every nation.

God continues his denunciation of the moral failure of the Babylonians. This arrogance also leads to them being 'never at rest'. That restless lack of peace may be contrasted with the Old Testament picture of peaceful *shalom*, in which the godly reside in the bosom of their family at home, sitting contentedly in the shade under their vine.

But puffed-up arrogance and immoral lack of uprightness is never content. It always wants more – and then yet more. Just as death and the grave (literally *Sheol*, the place of shades to which all the dead were sent in the Old Testament) continually claim new victims, so the Babylonians' greed is never satisfied. Conquest of one nation leads on to further campaigns against other peoples. They cannot stop until they have conquered the whole world and everyone in it. We may note the repeated *all* – not just 'more', but 'all the nations' and 'all the peoples'. Greed and conquest know no end. Evil cannot rest; it drives the wicked and the godless into ever further sin. The thief feels an inner compulsion to steal again. The murderer lusts after more blood. Sin never sits back in contented satisfaction, but always wants more – and still more.

In the midst of this description of the Babylonians' pride and moral sin comes an unexpected little addition to God's accusations against them: 'wine betrays him.'

Throughout the centuries and in all parts of the world the misuse of alcohol abounds in societies where the Lord is left out of consideration. Idolatry and its consequent immorality go hand-in-hand with drunkenness and a dependence on alcohol. A life of driving ambition, greed and ungodly behaviour needs the stimulus of drink to keep going. People assume that any success or happy event must be celebrated by consuming considerable quantities of alcohol. And the insecurity of a restless life without true concern for other people or nations requires alcohol to dull the senses. But the happiness and exuberance which comes from drinking is false and cannot satisfy, so God describes it as a betrayal. People think that alcoholic drink will give them happiness and a good time, but it is a lie. Reality returns the following morning.

When followers of Jesus hear this fearful description of the Babylonians' sin, we can only rejoice in the Lord's gift to us of his peace – and we praise him for it. Complaining gives way to confident joy. And then we come to him again, asking for that true spirit of contented *shalom*.

2:4: The righteous will live by his faith

'The just – by faith – shall live.' The three Hebrew words of this verse have deeply influenced the whole evolution of the Christian faith and the history of the church. They formed the bedrock of Paul's faith and theological development in the first century. Then in the heady days of the Reformation they spearheaded the revolution against the theology and practice of a corrupt Roman Catholic church. Since the Reformation they have been the central text for evangelical Christians whose Christian faith is built on the great truth that we are made righteous not by our own merit and good works, but rather by faith in the crucified and risen Jesus Christ.

But controversy has raged around the exact meaning of these words. In his old commentary on Habakkuk Keil affirms that it is the words 'by faith' which stand out with particular emphasis, while A.C. Jennings declares with equal confidence that the word 'live' should be stressed.[1] Perhaps it might be truer to the original text to say that all three words have equal importance.

There has also been some disagreement among scholars as to whether the words 'by faith' relate to the preceding 'the just' or to the following 'shall live'. Do we become just or righteous by faith? Or do the just live by faith? Or are both true – do we therefore become righteous through our faith and then also live by that same faith? The text itself may be understood in any of these three possible ways, so perhaps we would be wise to accept the third possibility and relate the 'by faith' both to how we become righteous and to our consequent living.

This verse in Habakkuk is quoted three times in the New Testament and we need at this stage to examine briefly how it is used in Romans 1:17, Galatians 3:11 and Hebrews 10:37.

a) Romans 1:17

Romans 1:16,17 stands as the foundation text which forms the basis for Paul's whole letter to the Romans. It leads immediately to Paul's assertion of the universality of sin. None of us is in a position to complain against God or to blame him.

Jews and Gentiles alike face the same problem and are equally under sin. He summarizes this in Romans

3:9–18. He then proceeds to underline that Jews and Gentiles enjoy the same solution to the problem of sin and are equally made righteous through faith in the crucified Jesus Christ.

This righteousness comes therefore by faith in Jesus, not through 'works of law'. The reformers understood this to mean that people can be considered righteous as a result of their faith, not by means of merit and good works. This stood in contrast to the contemporary Roman Catholic emphasis on salvation by good works. Of course it is true that no human being can gain adequate merit by our own virtue to satisfy the demands of the burningly holy God, the one whose eyes are too pure even to look on evil (Hab. 1:13). But still we need to ask whether this is what Paul was emphasizing in Romans.

Although this interpretation has reigned unchallenged in evangelical circles for many years, in more recent times biblical scholars have begun to look at Romans with different eyes. Some of us as Jewish Christians had questioned this interpretation already many years ago, because we realized that the Jewish religious context of the first century differed radically from the Roman Catholicism of the Reformation period. In traditional Judaism we relate to God because of his election of us as his people. He chose us and made us his own, giving us the covenant of Moses to confirm this relationship. As Jews we therefore boast in God's covenant, the Law or Torah. Of course as the people of the Law we are expected to obey the Law and do the works of Torah. This demand relates closely to the Christian belief that we are called to obey the word of the Lord once we are born again into a living faith in Jesus and relationship with him.

In celebrating the Passover Jews have always known that redemption through shed blood preceded the exodus from Egypt and the giving of the covenantal Law. So what does Paul mean when he affirms that the just shall live by faith? Some years ago the liberal Swedish theologian K. Stendhal taught that Paul was defending his call to be apostle to the Gentiles and showing that righteousness is given both to Jews and to Gentiles equally. While the Torah was given only to Israel, faith in Jesus Christ is available to all peoples. More recently this emphasis has been expounded particularly by E.P. Sanders and by J. Dunn in his Word Commentary on Romans.[2]

In Romans itself, as we have already noted, the first three chapters demonstrate the universality of sin with the conclusion that 'Jews and Gentiles alike are all under sin' (Rom. 3:9). The glorious reality that salvation, justification and redemption are available through the sacrificial death of Jesus Christ (Rom. 3:21–26) still leaves open the question of whether Jesus' atoning work is only available for Israel or if it is now for all peoples.

The answer to this question is given in Romans 3:28–30. We are justified by faith apart from works of law (3:28). While Luther rightly rejoiced in 'faith apart from works' because of his context of corrupt Roman Catholicism at that time, he failed to see the significance of 'the law'. He had extreme difficulty therefore in understanding how 3:29 is a natural consequence of the 3:28 affirmation – 'or is God the God of Jews only? Is he not the God of Gentiles too? Yes, of Gentiles too . . .' (3:29). The universal problem of sin thus leads on, in Paul's exposition, to the universal nature of God's salvation through faith in Jesus Christ.

Paul goes on to remind his readers that Abraham was also justified by faith and therefore is called to be 'heir of the world' (Rom. 4:13), not just of Israel. He has become the father of both the circumcised and the uncircumcised (4:11,12), the father 'of many nations'

(4:17,18), indeed the 'father of us all' (4:16). So Paul demonstrates that his call to be the apostle to the Gentiles fits well into a true biblical faith. Although he was a Jew of the Jews, he was chosen by God to 'call people from among all the Gentiles to the obedience that comes from faith' (1:5). The gospel is indeed the power of God for the salvation not only of Israel, but also of the Gentiles (1:16).

Habakkuk the prophet had problems understanding how the God of Israel could possibly use the evil Babylonians as his instruments. Does God really work among idolatrous Gentiles? God commanded Habakkuk to 'look at the nations' (1:5) and see what God is doing among the Gentiles. Now Paul shows that God not only uses Gentiles to fulfil his purposes, but even works on their behalf in salvation.

b) Galatians 3:11

In Galatians 3:11 Paul has the same aim in quoting Habakkuk 2:4. The context reminds us of the contrast between faith and the law, not just between faith and works (Gal. 3:12). Paul rejoices that Christ has redeemed us from the curse of the law and has become a curse for us as he took the penalty for our sin upon himself through his death on the cross. Paul then declares that this redemption has the purpose that 'the blessing given to Abraham might come to the Gentiles through Christ Jesus' (3:14). So we are *all* sons of God through faith in Christ Jesus (3:26). Because righteousness is granted to people by faith and not just by the Jewish Law, salvation is open to all. Whether we are Jew or Gentile, slave or free, male or female, God allows us equally to become 'Abraham's seed' (3:28,29).

c) Hebrews 10:38

In Paul's references to Habakkuk 2:4, faith comes as a decisive turning-point in life which allows righteousness to be imputed to us. He uses the once-for-all Aorist past tense to describe our justification, so that there is a definite starting line for the race of life. We put our faith in Jesus Christ and he gives us his righteousness, and so we have life in him. The just shall live by faith.

But the writer of Hebrews is perhaps closer to Habakkuk's meaning in his use of Habakkuk 2:4. In Habakkuk the word 'faith' could perhaps be better translated by our word 'faithfulness'. For the prophet there seems to be no obvious evidence that God's revelation will ever come to pass. It does indeed 'linger'. Judah persists in her violence, conflict and injustice for year after year. And the idolatrous and cruel Babylonians sweep through the nations triumphantly without any effective resistance. The prophet has therefore asked 'Is he to *keep* on emptying his net?' (Hab. 1:17) and he cries to the Lord *'how long* must I call for help?' But God reassures him that the righteous will live if they persist in faith. Faithfulness will be rewarded with true life.

So it is in Hebrews. 'You need to persevere so that when you have done the will of God, you will receive what he has promised' (Heb. 10:36). Hebrews warns its readers against the danger of failing to persevere in faith, slipping away from following the Lord. God will not be pleased with us if we 'shrink back' (10:38). But in faithful perseverance we are to live in confident hope. 'Faith is being sure of what we hope for and certain of what we do not see. This is what the ancients were commended for' (Heb. 11:1–2) and then we are treated to the famous catalogue of Old Testament heroes who persisted in confident faithfulness, believing that God's promises would be fulfilled in the future. They 'were all commended for their faith, yet none of them received what had been promised' (11:39).

It should perhaps be noted in passing that the writer to the Hebrews uses the Greek Septuagint translation of Habakkuk, in which 'he who is coming will come and will not delay'. While in the Hebrew it is God's revelation for which we must wait with patience, the Septuagint personalizes the revelation. The revealed promises of God come to us in the person of the long-awaited Messiah. The revealed word has become the incarnate Word.

Still today as Christians we are called upon to continue in faith, even if there sometimes seems little evidence of God's kingdom coming. Faith and faithfulness find their rest on the pillow of God's promises. Jesus will surely come again and his perfect kingdom will surely be established. So let us continue to run the race that is set before us. The righteous will indeed *live* by their faith and their faithfulness.

We may note the clear link between this verse and 1:12. Resting on the assured fact that God is eternally 'from everlasting', the prophet states with confident faith that 'we will not die'. This assurance defies the apparent danger that the Babylonians might well kill the people they defeat so cruelly. Does the prophet believe that he himself and other righteous ones among God's people will be kept alive in the midst of all the destruction? Or is the prophet reminding the Lord of his covenant promises to Israel and therefore reaffirming his confidence that these promises cannot be denied? His election is sure. God's purposes for Israel will undoubtedly come to pass. Remembering God's loving election of his people Israel, Paul would later echo the same assurance that 'God's gifts and his call are irrevocable'

(Rom. 11:29). So Paul cannot doubt that he 'will turn godlessness away from Jacob' (Rom. 11:26), God's mercies will surely come to Jews as well as to Gentiles (Rom. 11:25,26,30–32) and finally 'all Israel will be saved' (Rom. 11:26). As Jewish Christians we look forward joyfully to the fulfilment of this glorious promise of God. However hard and relatively unresponsive evangelism among Jewish people may appear to be, we maintain this confidence as our aim and purpose.

Five

God's Solution – God's Justice Prevails

Habakkuk 2:5–20

At last Habakkuk is given God's final answer. Now we come to God's solution to the prophet's queries and problems. In this section the Lord demonstrates his absolute righteousness, and his justice is vindicated. Sin will not always prevail, but judgment will come. And the people of God will in the end be saved from the suffering which an evil nation is inflicting upon them at present. But the most important element in the Lord's final revealed purpose is neither the judgment of sinners nor the salvation of God's people. The climax of everything lies rather in the glorification of the Lord himself. His great name will be uplifted and all the world will acknowledge his supremacy (see also Phil. 2:10,11; Col. 1:18).

In the Bible the twin concepts of judgment and salvation represent the two sides of one coin. God's outpoured grace towards those who repent and turn to him in faith is matched by his righteous judgment of unrepentant sinners. We may follow Martin Luther in calling this situation the right and left hands of God. Both hands work simultaneously and we cannot have the one without the other. Just as light can only be enjoyed when in contrast with darkness, so grace and salvation fill us with thanksgiving because of the fearful contrast with condemnation and judgment. It is the holiness of God in his burning purity which makes judgment a necessary outworking of his perfect justice. But at the same time his love runs with outstretched arms to welcome the repentant prodigal son or daughter. So our complaints against God seem trivial in comparison with his glorious grace.

God's grace towards repentant sinners is a unique feature of the biblical revelation. In other religions the creator god may show mercy towards those who are good and who follow his ways. But in the Bible we see that God lavishes his grace even on sinners. 'While we were still sinners, Christ died for us' (Rom. 5:8). 'We love because he first loved us' (1 Jn. 4:19). The glorious truth of God's totally undeserved grace has no parallel in any other religious faith. It is unique. And it is the foundation of all true biblical faith.

But we must never forget that God's grace remains inseparably linked to his total holiness and therefore also to his fearful judgment. Liberal theology has sought to obscure the awesome nature of God's righteous judgment and in doing so has often lost touch with the absolute holiness of God. An unbalanced emphasis on the loving mercy of God has prevailed. But, as the Japanese missiologist K. Kitamori has vividly described,[1] love and holy wrath combine in the nature of God. He points out how love without holiness becomes shallow and soft with a cloying sweetness. On the other hand, holy wrath without love horrifies us with its uncaring judgmental harshness. In our appreciation of the character and nature of God, the biblical revelation with its combination of loving grace with righteous judgment must be kept without one-sided compromise. Habakkuk 2:5–20 maintains this wholeness as it declares God's final purposes.

In 1:17 the Babylonians are seen to be destroying one nation after another without end. And in 2:5 they bring all the nations under their merciless rule and take all the peoples captive. Now in 2:6 the tables are turned, the biter is bitten in his turn. '*All of them* taunt him with ridicule and scorn'. *All* are tormented by the Babylonians, *all* now turn on their cruel oppressors and so *all* the earth bows in silence before the sovereign glory of God (2:20). In this context one is tempted to add to the well-known words of final victory in 2:14 and say too that *all* the earth will be filled with the knowledge of the glory of God. Just as all the surrounding nations had suffered under the hand of the Babylonians, so now all the nations join gladly in God's judgment of their enemy.

Many persecuted Christians will take comfort in this passage. Suffering at the hands of powerful anti-Christian police or governments, they await the final vindication of their Lord, demonstrating that the faith for which they are suffering really is God's truth. They dare not take vengeance themselves against those who abuse them so terribly, but they look for the time when God's righteous judgment will be evident. We are reminded of God's assurance that 'it is mine to avenge; I will repay' (Rom. 12:19), but this verse comes in the context of God's command that we should live at peace with everyone. We must never take revenge on people however cruelly they treat us. We are called to 'overcome evil with good' (Rom. 12:21).

In 2:6 the NIV's 'taunt', 'ridicule' and 'scorn' translate three particular Hebrew words. The first is *mashal*, which commonly means a parable or proverbial expression. So we are not surprised, as we study the following passage more closely, that it includes considerable poetic language and onomatopoeia. This was also true of God's first description of the Babylonians in 1:6–10 in which God uses vivid imagery to paint a picture of the terrifying advance of the hostile army. Again, onomatopoeia plays a significant part in these verses together with the fearful imagery of leopards, wolves and vultures swooping on their defenceless prey. Likewise the imagery in 2:6–20 is evocatively expressive, but it should not be taken too literally. In reading the Bible we always need to distinguish between sections which are clearly parabolic or symbolic and should not be interpreted literally word for word, while other passages are obviously intended as accurate declarations of truth or historical fact. Both the original writers and those for whom they were writing would have known the difference between the parabolic or poetic and definite affirmations of historical or doctrinal truth.

The second of the words used here in 2:6 is rightly translated in the NIV as 'ridicule', for it has a sense of mocking derision. Again we see how God's judgment fits the evil of the Babylonians. In 1:10 it was noted that 'they deride kings and scoff at rulers. They laugh at all fortified cities'. Now in their turn they will become the object of the nations' mockery as God's judgment demonstrates how pathetic and puny even the Babylonians are when confronted with the mighty power of almighty God. When God judges people, they are often moved to blame God for their misfortune. But actually the judgments of God demonstrate an amazing appropriateness.

As we observe today the seemingly invincible power of nations and ideologies, we shall be encouraged by this reminder that God stands in glory above every evil power. In comparison with him they are as nothing. The glorious cross, resurrection and ascension of Jesus Christ has already defeated Satan and all his minions, so we look with confidence to the final judgment. Then the Lord and his people will triumph and those who oppose him in unrepentant evil and pride shall be brought low. We know that God has already 'disarmed the powers and authorities' and has 'made a public spectacle of them, triumphing over them by the cross' (Col. 2:15). Just as the kingdom of God has come and yet we still pray 'your kingdom come', so likewise we wait expectantly for the day when God's victory over all evil will finally be fully realized. Then the Babylonians' modern equivalents will be humbled before the Lord and in the eyes of God's people.

The third word used in 2:6 (*chidot*) means 'riddles'. It is used, for example, in Judges 14 of Samson's riddle concerning honey in the lion's carcass. Does this refer back to all the questions which Habakkuk had presented to God? The prophet had been wracked with deep doubts concerning what God was doing and why. He could not reconcile God's working with his fundamental character and nature. It was as if God was facing him with fearful riddles. Or perhaps this word 'riddles' relates rather to what God will do in the final judgment. Will the Babylonians be bewildered by their humiliation in the eyes of all the nations and fail utterly to understand what God is doing? Will all the utterances of 'woe' in this passage seem like riddles in the Babylonians' minds?

In any case, it is certain that Habakkuk has been eagerly awaiting a clear answer from the Lord to all his questionings. And now at last God explains what his ultimate purposes are, and how his righteousness and justice will finally be vindicated. In the end God will ensure that everything comes right. Widespread salvation will penetrate not only into all Judah, but far into all the world. The idolatrous and cruel Babylonians will be judged and all the world will see that God does work righteously. And all the earth will be struck dumb in awe-filled silence as they see the splendour of God's kingdom reign (2:20). What a vision! Surely this is God's revelation not only for Habakkuk, Judah and the people of that time. This is God's answer to all our complaints. It is a word for all people of all backgrounds everywhere, throughout the ups and downs of history.

While it is the plural 'all of them' who taunt the Babylonians with 'ridicule and scorn', 2:6 then continues with the singular 'he'. Commentaries vary in their inter-pretation of who this 'he' may refer to. Is it the righteous one who lives by faith (2:4)? Or is it implying that in their scorn for the Babylonians all the nations are speaking in unity as one person? It is a sad truth that when affliction falls on people the world unites in its criticism against them.

We need to look in more detail at this great passage of Scripture. The structure of this passage is formed around five denunciations of the Babylonians, the first four of which start with the expression 'Woe to him who . . .' The final denunciation changes the order to underline its par-ticular importance as the climax of their evil. In this fifth word of condemnation (2:18–20) the words 'Woe to him who . . .' (2:19) come right in the middle.

In the midst of this fearful catalogue of Babylonian sin and judgement we find two golden nuggets of positive grace and blessing. We shall examine in detail the well-known words of 2:14 that 'the earth will be filled with the knowledge of the glory of the Lord, as the waters cover the sea'. What a source of praise and joyful expec-tation these words represent in the midst of such a series of expressions of 'woe' with the tragic reality of God's holy judgment! And then, right at the end of the chapter as its final climax, comes the reminder that in all situations and at all times 'the Lord is in his holy temple' with its consequent declaration 'let all the earth be silent before him'. In everything God himself retains his absolute authority. He is in control. All human complaints or objections fall silent when we stand before the glorious sovereignty of the living God.

The first woe (2:6–8)

This first 'woe' not only condemns the Babylonians themselves, but starts with a more generalized truth. Anyone who gains wealth by unjust or violent means will finally receive their just condemnation. As O. Palmer Robertson comments in his commentary on Habakkuk, 'piles up' or 'multiplies' reminds the reader of various statements in Proverbs, particularly Proverbs 22:16 'He who oppresses the poor to increase his wealth and he who gives gifts to the rich – both come to poverty.'

How apt this word is for our contemporary world scene where so often political leaders use their power to feather their own nests at the expense of the poor and the weak. Corruption seems at first to pay handsome dividends, but we may be assured that the justice of God will finally strike.

We cannot blame God for such people's evil. In fact God shows that he so hates such injustice and cruelty that he will judge them accordingly.

These words about multiplying stolen goods underline the way evil people can never rest content with the wealth they have accumulated, but always long for yet more and more. Ill-gotten gains never allow people to relax and enjoy what they have. They are driven by a burning inner compulsion to go on piling up their riches.

So the question comes again, 'How long?' (2:6). In 1:2 the prophet had asked how long he must go on calling for help in the midst of the violence and sin of his own people Judah. In 1:17 he had then asked God whether the Babylonians were to 'keep on' emptying their nets and destroying nations without mercy. Now, in spite of the Lord's assurance that God's purposes 'will certainly come and will not delay' (2:3), the question arises again. How long will the Babylonians go on accumulating their ever-increasing abundance of stolen goods?

It had appeared that the Babylonians were invincible, and there seemed no end to their conquering might. But the end comes abruptly in verse seven. Judgment will break onto the scene with abrupt and unexpected suddenness. To the utter amazement of all, those who were suffering under the cruelty of the Babylonians will 'suddenly arise'. The down and outs will experience a sudden resurrection. In the NIV the defeated nations are called 'debtors' which has the possible translation 'creditors' in the footnote. Actually, the original Hebrew means 'those who bite'. These many peoples had been badly bitten by the Babylonians, but now they will suddenly arise and bite the Babylonians. The biter will be bitten. God's judgment is fearfully appropriate. As they did to others, so it will be done to them. Likewise in 2:8 they 'plundered many nations', but now they in their turn will be plundered. They have destroyed rural lands, urban cities and the people – a comprehensive list which just emphasizes the completeness of the Babylonians' vicious destruction of all around them. But now God's judgment is coming. God will no longer 'raise up the Babylonians' (1:6), but he will cause the defeated nations to arise and the Babylonians will become their victims (2:7). The holy

God is indeed totally just and righteous in all his judgments. He demonstrates that he stands above all our complaints.

The second woe (2:9–11)

In the first 'woe' God warns that his righteous judgment will fall on the Babylonians in a way that fits their sins. Now the second 'woe' comes upon them despite their desperate attempts to make themselves secure against all possible attack. Like a bird building its nest in a remote unreachable place, so the Babylonians locate their centres in strongly defended positions – they 'set [their] nest on high, to escape the clutches of ruin' (2:9). But God's threatened 'woe' is inescapable! He is determined to show that the prophet's complaints against him were misplaced – he is totally just in his judgments.

As in the first 'woe', so here too the prophet's use of language is very evocative. Perhaps the prophet was thinking of Psalm 33:16 with its assurance that 'no king is saved by the size of his army; no warrior escapes by his great strength'. Habakkuk had complained that the people of God were suffering at the hands of the evil Babylonians, but now that complaint is answered – they will not escape the clutches of similar evil. The same basic word for 'evil' is used twice in verse nine, translated in the NIV as 'unjust' and 'ruin'. It is indeed the Babylonians, not God, who are to be blamed for what is evil!

The word 'house' is also repeated to emphasize the Babylonians' attempts to find security by building their house like a nest, but actually they are bringing shame to their own house (2:10). We all desire domestic security, but sin in society always leads to the breakdown of family life and therefore shame in areas of life which should be private and secure. In Britain we know this only too well – and we cannot blame God for it!

The words translated 'builds' and 'gain' in 2:9 really mean 'covet',[2] for even the Babylonians' domestic life is marked by covetousness. People constantly long to possess what their neighbour already has, so they covet better and better houses with more and more of the latest gadgetry. Such sin destroys God's purposes for us: domestic contentment with interpersonal peace and harmony. With our fallen natures we are so easily led astray by the bombardment of advertisements which assure us that 'we deserve . . .'

So the prophet concludes this 'woe' with a dialogue between the very stones and beams of their houses. In 1:2 the prophet was 'crying out' to a seemingly inactive God that he was surrounded by Judah's violence and wickedness, but now it is the very 'stones of the wall' which cry out in agony at God's judgment and the 'beams of the woodwork' answer back like an echo. The very structures of the Babylonians' homes call out in distress, for shame has fallen on their houses.

In plotting the downfall of many other nations, they have sown the seeds for their own destruction. In history we see how conquering empires always fall eventually into disastrous ruin. The peoples they subdue finally rise up against them, demand their independence and vengeance on their former oppressors. Habakkuk points out that the consequence is shame on their house and the forfeiture of their life (literally 'soul'). In the earlier sections of the book the prophet had complained to God about his apparent failures, but now it is clear that the shame belongs only to those who bring harm to others.

The third woe (2:12–14)

In the previous 'woe' Habakkuk had complained that the Babylonians had tried desperately to build security into their national life. Now he notes that they built their secure city and town through the shedding of blood and through evil or iniquity (2:12). With considerable bloodshed they have destroyed cities (2:8) and now the complaints of the prophet are matched by the fitting judgment of God. The finger of God is pointed against the Babylonians because of their murderous bloodletting and their evil towards the different nations. As David Baker says in his Tyndale commentary, 'all of the effort of building and self-aggrandizement will be of no lasting value and will literally go up in smoke'.

The Lord's reply to Habakkuk's complaints now leads on to widely applicable general principles. These apply first to God's own people, but also to 'the nations' (2:13). In the light of the prophet's first complaint in 1:1–4 God declares that Israel's 'labour is only fuel for the fire'. All that the people of Israel and Judah may seek to do leads only to judgment. They weary themselves in all their evildoing and in all their conflicts with each other, but it all just adds fuel to God's fire of judgment.

Exactly the same is true for the wider world of the Gentiles, the nations. They spend themselves in exhausting warfare in their desire to conquer the world, but all their effort is 'for nothing'. We are reminded of the book of Ecclesiastes with its depressing description of life without the Lord – 'all is meaningless' (Ecc. 1:2).[3] Many in today's world would echo these words in their hearts. Life appears to them a senselessly empty round of working to live and living to work. It seems to have no meaningful purpose. And many will blame God for allowing life to remain as an exhausting round of emptiness. Like the nations in 2:13 people still today 'exhaust them-selves' in frenetic activity and long hours at work, so that they live their lives in a state of constant tiredness. And yet it still proceeds without any worthwhile goal. And the wearier they become, the more they may feel that it is God's fault!

While it is true that Israel's 'labour is only fuel for the fire' and the Gentile nations 'exhaust themselves for nothing', God directs the world's history with a definite purpose and goal. These two verses of 2:13,14 highlight the stark contrast between the aimless life of godless people and the fixed purpose of God. God's history moves firmly forwards to its climax, in which 'the earth will be filled with the knowledge of the glory of the Lord'. We shall look in detail at this verse later.

The fourth woe (2:15–17)

Having observed the tragedy of both Judah's and the Babylonians' emptiness of life despite their desperate frenetic activity, Habakkuk now faces the dark side of their lives. The national life of both Judah and the Babylonians was characterized by violence. Now we see what that violence led up to. We have already seen that in contrast to the life of faith and righteousness, 'wine betrays him' (2:5). Now in 2:15 this is further described. They purposely make their neighbours drunk for their own amusement with no regard for others' welfare. They bring their neighbour into the shame of immodest nakedness. Sexual prurience and lust have taken over.

In his commentary O. Palmer Robertson rightly points out that this verse points not only to indecent exposure, but to actual practice of sexual sin. Indeed he suggests that 'very possibly the reference is to a homosexual act'.

When we read the descriptions in 2:15 it seems extreme. But sadly many of us will recognize such behaviour as common in Europe today. Students and young people enjoy making their friends get drunk. Sexual lust and sin follow naturally. Like the prophet we too feel indignant before God that the beauty of sex has been contaminated and corrupted by its perversion. We seem to live in an age when sex and its misuse dominate the media and people's thinking.

Sexual lewdness brings shame to all who indulge in it. But God declares that those who bring others into shame will themselves be put to shame (2:16). They may have exulted in mocking people who they have led into drunken nakedness, but now they too 'will be filled with shame'. Once again God's judgment is absolutely fitting and appropriate. The double use of 'glory' underlines the Babylonians' pride. As they enjoy laughing at others, they bolster their own self-glory and think they are so big. 'Where is God in all this shocking evil?' the prophet might well have asked. But the righteous need not worry too much, for God's hand of holy judgment will now fall and disgrace will cover their arrogant self-glorification. Justice will reign.

So Habakkuk 2:17 summarizes with the assurance that the Babylonians' violence (the same word as in 1:2,3,9; 2:8) will overwhelm them in their turn. The twofold repetition of the word 'violence' reminds us of the central nature of this characteristic in the sin both of Judah and of the Babylonians. Throughout history, in every society, violence takes over when godless sin prevails.

We may be surprised by the statement that Babylon is judged for their violence against Lebanon, and not particularly for what they did to Judah and to Jerusalem. Is this because Lebanon was known for its gentle beauty? To despoil beauty is especially horrifying. In modern times too we are particularly offended by the destruction of artistic treasures or places of beauty.

Likewise we may feel that God's emphasis on the sin of 'destruction of animals' is wrong. Surely people are more important than animals! It is of course perverse to be more concerned for animals than for human beings. But our treatment of defenceless flora and fauna demonstrates what sort of people we are. Cruelty towards animals shows how low people have fallen.

In the world of our day it is vitally important for the whole future of the universe that we treat the created world with dignity and not with a casual or cruel lack of care. We need always to remember that the world is created by God and indeed exists for the sake of the Lord's pleasure, not just ours (Col. 1:16). God's purposes embrace the natural world as well as humanity, so that we look for the day when there will be a new heaven and a new earth as well as a new humanity.

So God lumps everything together in the final words of these three verses: violence towards Lebanon, destruction of animals, shedding the blood of men and women, destroying lands, cities and 'everyone in them' (2:17). Sin is all-embracing in its devastating impact.

The fifth and final woe (2:18–20)

The climax of the Lord's answer to Habakkuk's complaints denounces the Babylonians' idolatry. Once again we note how moral sin and religious sin go hand-in-hand together. False belief and religious practice will always lead to moral iniquity. And in God's denunciation of the Babylonians the climax lies in their worship of idols.

Like the psalmist in Psalm 115 this passage has no hesitation in showing the total vanity of the Babylonians' religion. Their idols have no value because they are just man-made objects. As such they are lifeless. Indeed, in so far as they do communicate at all they 'teach lies'. But actually they 'cannot speak'. And their very existence imparts to their worshippers false values even if they have 'no breath in them'. Habakkuk describes the idols as *elilim*, a diminutive and dismissive term. As Christopher Wright says in his monumental *The Mission of God*, this term refers 'to something worthless, weak, powerless, useless, of no value'.[4]

In his answer to Habakkuk God does not hesitate to mock such false worship. It is ridiculous to beg mere wood to 'come to life' or to say to lifeless stone 'Wake up!' (2:19). It may look beautiful with its covering of gold and silver, but it still remains just wood or stone carved by human hands. It cannot 'give guidance'.

God's mockery of the Babylonians' false religion as recorded here in Habakkuk stands in stark contrast to what is politically correct today. Such words would be considered unacceptably intolerant and might even be illegal in many European countries. But God does not mince his words in declaring what is right and true, even if it appears very negative.

Isaiah 44:6–23 may be paralleled to these three verses in Habakkuk. Isaiah too mocks the foolishness of carving an idol out of half a tree while using the other half for firewood. So he asks the laughable question, 'Shall I bow down to a block of wood?' (Is. 44:19).The contrast between man-made idols and the living God is mind-blowing. Both Isaiah and Habakkuk make this abundantly clear. While the idols remain dumb with no life in them, God rules supreme in his world. Indeed the climax of this whole chapter rings out with assured confidence: 'The Lord is in his holy temple; let all the earth be silent before him'.

The idols cannot speak and must remain silent. Now all the earth should likewise remain silent in the presence of the glory of God. All Habakkuk's complaints come to an end as he faces the sovereign majesty and holiness of the all-glorious living God.

Christians too need sometimes to be reminded of the burning purity and holiness of the God we worship. There is always a danger that we come too lightly and easily into his presence. We also talk and sing too much. We might do better to remain silent from time to time in order to allow God to do the talking! The awesome reality of his holy presence should move us to respectful silence.

Six

Filled With the Knowledge of His Glory – Nothing To Complain About

Habakkuk 2:14

The prophetic book of Habakkuk started off with his first complaint as he observed the fearful evil and corruption which ruled in Judah, the covenant people of God. Why didn't God do something in that situation? Surely the righteous heart of God should have been moved to bring reformation and revival. But it seemed that God sat idly by and was ignoring the desperate prayers of his prophet.

But God replied and informed Habakkuk that he was actually very active, but not in the way the prophet was expecting. He was not renewing Judah, but working among the despised Gentiles. He was raising up the Babylonians as his instruments.

That led naturally to Habakkuk's second complaint against God. How could the all-holy God deal with such barbarously cruel and idolatrous people as the Babylonians? The very character of God in his absolute perfection and purity was at stake. So the prophet blamed God for doing what seemed unrighteous. But Habakkuk is not content just to voice his objections. He sets himself to seek a definite answer from God.

In our last chapter we saw God's reply to Habakkuk's accusations against him. God will not allow his justice to be impugned. He is totally righteous and just. The Babylonians will be judged and God delivers a fearful list of 'woes' in accusation and judgment against the Babylonians. And the second chapter concludes with the triumphant affirmation that God rules with holy justice, so all complaints are silenced in his awesome presence.

In the midst of the negative wilderness of judgment in the catalogue of 'woes' comes the golden nugget of 2:14. Although God was particularly answering Habakkuk's complaints and therefore revealing his ultimate purposes of just judgment, he especially loves to demonstrate his grace and love. His righteous character is not only seen in negative judgment, but also more wonderfully in the positive glorification of his name and salvation of his people.

'The earth'

In the first chapters of Genesis we read that God created the heavens and 'the earth'. This word refers therefore not to one small part of the world, but to the whole created universe. As history unfolded, the Hebrew word for 'the earth' (*erets*) came to be associated with the 'land' of Israel (*erets* Israel). So in chapter one of his Gospel John carefully changes the Genesis creation word 'earth' and uses the word 'world' (Jn. 1:9–10). He repeats the word 'world' four times in quick succession to underline the fact that Jesus was incarnate in this world not just for the sake of his people Israel, but for the whole world. Christians therefore must also always maintain a mission vision for all peoples everywhere.

In Habakkuk 2:20 'all the earth' fell silent before the living Lord in his sovereign reign over all. So now too in 2:14 'the earth' surely signifies the totality of all the world. With some justification therefore we might be permitted to add the word 'all' – all the earth will be filled with the knowledge of the glory of the Lord. Martin Luther set us an example in adding a word to underline the real meaning of Scripture when he affirmed that we are justified not just by faith, but by 'faith alone' (*sola fide*).

As Christians we eagerly look forward to this climactic pinnacle of God's answer to all our questions and complaints. Everywhere will know his glory – every country, every town and even every village. Each of us can think of where we personally live or work – this place and this country will be filled with the knowledge of his glory. It is almost beyond our powers of imagination to picture such an awesome outworking of human history. We remember God's word to Habakkuk, 'I am doing something in your days that you would not believe, even if you were told.'

What an incentive for dynamic involvement in worldwide mission! We link ourselves to the very working of God himself in sharing his glory with all people in all the earth.

'Will be filled'

Clearly this verse is not talking of some small movement among the peoples of the world. The word 'filled' assumes a large scale development, in which the whole earth will be characterized by a significant revelation of the knowledge of the glory of the Lord. Many of us as Christians have grown accustomed to being satisfied with a little group of believers here and there. But God's desire remains for a mass turning of people from the empty vanity of godlessness and wickedness to a knowledge of the glory of God. He will not be content with anything less than a mass movement to a saving knowledge of Christ in every part of the world.

The word 'filled' reminds us of Romans 11:25 and 26. Parallel to the purposes of God revealed in Habakkuk 2:14, Paul's vision also extends to the day when 'the full number' of the Gentiles will come in and when 'all Israel' will be saved. The *pleroma* (fullness) of the Gentiles would seem to go together with 'all' Israel. Both 'fullness' and 'all' would seem to indicate a large number, but not every individual. Paul is not envisaging universal salvation of every person without exception, for salvation still depends on faith in Jesus Christ and some will always reject him. But he is foreseeing the day when there will be a massive turning to God of people from every nation and tongue. Surely this vision goes naturally together with the picture in Revelation 7:9 of 'a great multitude that no one could count, from every nation, tribe, people and language'. Crowds of Jews and Gentiles of every nation and background will fall down on their faces before the throne and worship God (Rev. 7:11). This is the goal of Christian mission and it is God's goal and purpose for every Christian and church. As fellow-workers with Christ we pray and work to bring this purpose of God into reality. Hasten the day when the multitudes of all nations and peoples will love, worship and serve the Lord!

Before this verse in Romans 11 Paul has talked of the olive tree of Israel having some of its branches cut off because of their unbelief, but then new Gentile branches are added. Finally the natural Jewish branches will also be re-grafted back into that same tree of Israel. So the olive tree which at the outset was purely Jewish has Gentile branches incorporated into it. Then it has a multitude of Jewish branches brought back into its life. So finally the olive tree of Israel has the fullness of both Jews and Gentiles enjoying the glory of God's covenant grace and love.

We may note in passing that Paul does not say that the whole tree was cut down and replaced by a new tree. It is always the same olive tree of Israel which continues on into the final days when both Jews and Gentiles of every nation will belong. Careless and inaccurate talk of Pentecost as the birthday of the church is biblically inaccurate and untrue. The church[1] is the covenant people of Israel, but it has now widened out in the new covenant in Jesus to include people of every background.

We look forward to that day when crowds of people in every country, town and village of every continent will rejoice in the knowledge of the glory of our Lord Jesus. There certainly won't be any grumbling then!

'Knowledge'

In modern English the word 'knowledge' has come to mean a mere intellectual understanding of something. But in the Hebrew it meant much more than this. It implies a deep relationship at every level of one's being. It is not only academic and intellectual, concerned only with the use of the mind. It includes also a spiritual and emotional relationship; so that one is closely intertwined in one's whole being with that which one knows. It is even used as a euphemism for sexual relations between husband and wife. It is frequently said in the Old Testament that 'a man *knows* his wife'. So it describes that most intimate act of inter-personal relationship which involves the totality of the man's and the woman's whole nature.

Indeed, God's relationship with his people Israel in the Old Testament is often described with the language of marriage. We may see this very particularly in the book of Hosea, but it is found again and again throughout the Old Testament. And it continues into the New Testament in its picture of God's relationship with the church as his bride (Eph. 5:25; Rev. 22:17) and Jesus' relationship with each one of us as his followers.

It is the unique privilege of Christians that through the cross, resurrection and ascension of Jesus we are welcomed into such a close personal knowledge of God the Father. No other faith can match this deep personal knowledge of the almighty God which Jesus has opened up for us. And what a privilege it is that weak little sinners like us are not only permitted into the presence of God, but warmly welcomed. Such undeserved grace surely moves us to respond in love, gratitude and worship.

And this is God's purpose for all people and all peoples. He has as his goal for human history that the whole earth will be filled with the knowledge of his glory. In the creation God had an unclouded and intimate personal relationship with Adam and Eve, so that before sin entered in they could walk in harmony and love together through the garden in the cool of the evening. Sadly the curse of sin destroyed that harmonious knowledge of God, but through the redeeming work of Christ it has been restored and will ultimately climax in the perfection of glory when we shall *know* the Lord even as he *knows* us. And this knowledge of God's glory will spread into every corner of the world in every land, so that it fills the whole earth. What an incentive to get involved in worldwide mission!

'The glory'

While in the book of Habakkuk God promises that the earth will be filled with the knowledge of *the glory* of the Lord, Isaiah omits the words 'the glory' (Is. 11:9). Commentators debate whether Habakkuk was following Isaiah in quoting this verse or whether Isaiah took the words from Habakkuk. Did Habakkuk add 'the glory' to the words of Isaiah and, if so, why? Or did Isaiah take Habakkuk's words and leave 'the glory' out – and if so, why? Perhaps we shall never know which prophet came first and which was quoting from the other. But at least we can ask ourselves why Habakkuk includes 'the glory' and why Isaiah leaves it out.

In Isaiah the prophet is foreseeing the time when the Messiah will come to judge the world and to bring his peace. Like Habakkuk he too underlines the holy righteousness of God and therefore the reality of the ultimate judgment (Is. 11:3–5), but the immediate context of 11:9 is the beautiful picture of the wolf living together with the lamb, the leopard lying down with the goat, the lion eating straw like the ox and the young child putting his hand with total safety into the viper's nest (11:6–8). Isaiah's climax is that the whole earth will be full of the knowledge of the Lord. Any reminder of the blazing purity of the unapproachable glory of the Lord would introduce a jarring note into this wonderful picture of harmonious peace.

On the other hand, as we have seen, Habakkuk 2:14 comes in the midst of a fearful picture of God's holiness in action in judging the Babylonians. A reminder to his readers of the absolute glory and burning holiness of the almighty God fits exactly into this context. And yet the verse does not only concentrate on the unapproachable glory of God, but also on the positive promise that the

earth will relate intimately to that very glory of God. All
the world and everyone in it will *know* God's glory personally.

The concept of 'glory' in the Old Testament always
has both God's transcendent majesty and his immanent
presence in mind. When the Old Testament speaks of
God's glory it is referring to the absolute splendour of
God, but the splendour is revealed to his people and
resides in their midst. We may see an example of this in
the wilderness wanderings of Israel after the exodus
from Egypt and before they enter into the Promised
Land. God's glory takes its place in the very centre of the
people when they are encamped at night, but also leads
them from the front in the daytime. This parallels the
kings of the surrounding nations who also encamped at
night in the centre of their people, but led them from the
front when they were marching forwards in the daytime.
God was Israel's king and still today he remains our
king, who is with us as Immanuel and who leads us step
by step through life.

So in the midst of that terrible list of woes with the
fearful prospect of God's holy and just judgment, we
eagerly look forward to that wonderful day when all the
world will in the full sense of the word *know* the glory of
the Lord.

'Of the Lord'

As one who was a missionary and who now teaches mission, I am often asked what the ultimate purpose and
goal of mission should be. Many assume that mission is
particularly aimed at the salvation of men and women. It
consists primarily therefore of evangelistic preaching.
People then quickly add that mission should also

include many other activities and aims in terms of edifying God's church, serving the social needs of suffering humanity and beautifying the natural world with ecological care. All such activities should indeed form part of the work of the church's mission in the world. But the primary purpose of God's church and people must always remain the same, namely that the Lord should be glorified. The Old Testament repeatedly reminds us that God's working is 'not for your sake, but for my name's sake'. We live and work for the glory and honour of the Lord, not just for the welfare of humanity or the benefit of the natural world.

In the Bible the first command is that we should love the Lord our God with all that we are and all that we have. Love always longs for the other to be honoured. A loving husband or wife is delighted when people say nice things about their spouse. And, of course, the surest way to alienate a husband or wife is to criticize their beloved. Similarly, all good parents love to see their children praised and given prominence. They purr with delight when their child's teacher gives a glowing report or when their child is given a lead part in the school play or wins a place in a sports team.

In the same way, as those who love the Lord we long for the name of our beloved Lord to be praised and honoured as he deserves. That must be our primary aim in life. And we feel deeply saddened when we see that the Lord is ignored, misunderstood or blasphemed.

It is therefore helpful that Habakkuk 2:14 reminds us that it is *the Lord's* glory which is the ultimate goal of history. His glory will fill the earth and all will see and acknowledge it. We are reminded of the well-known promise in Philippians 2:9–11. In these verses we cannot but be impressed by the threefold repetition of the word 'every'. God has given Jesus 'the name that is above *every*

name, that at the name of Jesus *every* knee should bow
. . . and *every* tongue confess that Jesus Christ is Lord'.
The Buddha, Krishna, Mohammed, Moses – none of
them can at all be compared with the glory of Jesus
Christ. He is unique in the glory of who he is and what
he has done for us all.

It is, however, noteworthy that God the Father has so
exalted Jesus because he was willing to renounce his
heavenly splendour and his equality with God, taking
the form of a slave and humbling himself even unto
death on the cross. In Milton's *Paradise Lost* Satan
declares that it is better to reign in Hell than to serve in
Heaven, but Jesus gives his people exactly the opposite
model. He comes in humility to serve.

Paul shows in this passage that such Christ-like
humility forms the foundation for Christians to be 'like-
minded, having the same love, being one in spirit and
purpose' (Phil. 2:2). Was he thinking of the two women,
Euodia and Syntyche, who were quarrelling in disagreement with each other? (Phil. 4:2). Such unhappy relations deny the very heart of the gospel of Jesus Christ
because they fail to manifest love, peace, forgiveness and
reconciliation. How then can we preach the gospel when
we deny it by our unloving relationships within the
church?

So as Christians we are challenged to pray, live and
work for the glory of the Lord. This is God's ultimate
aim for us and for world history. It is his assured promise that finally the whole earth will be filled with the
knowledge of his glory. As our thinking and dreaming
become more and more aligned with the very mind of
Christ, so we shall increasingly share God's purpose that
Jesus may be honoured and glorified as he deserves to
be. That is God's purpose and it is to be our purpose in
life.

'As the waters cover the sea'

It is very possible that the expression 'as the waters cover the sea' was a common proverb to underline the totality of what precedes it. So it comes both here and in the parallel passage in Isaiah 11 in order to further emphasize that God's promise in this verse really will come to pass. We are encouraged to believe with confident faith that God will indeed reveal the fullness of his glory to all people everywhere. The whole world will come into the knowledge of God's glory. When we are faced with the majority of our population rejecting the good news of Jesus Christ and turning their backs on God, we may stand firm on God's assured promise in this verse. We can put to one side all our negativity concerning the possibility of our churches growing and the crowds coming to follow Jesus. The multitudes will learn to know the Messiah Jesus and through him the glory of God the Father.

In Habakkuk 3:10 and 3:15 we see that the movement of the waters stands entirely under the controlling hand of almighty God. The torrents of water sweep by and the waves are lifted on high at the Lord's command. It was God who 'trampled the sea' with his horses and caused the great waters to churn and seethe. For the people of Israel the sea was always an uncontrollable enemy, so it is particularly significant when Habakkuk confesses that God rules sovereignly over the sea. In the creation account it was the Spirit of God who 'was hovering over the waters' (Gen. 1:2), and God who determined the extent of the waters 'to separate water from water', 'he gathered the waters and called them "seas" (Gen. 1:10).' Right from the outset of world history God ruled over the waters and the seas. God still reigns today even over what is most apparently threatening and chaotic.

Together with Habakkuk, Christians today can look forward with confidence to the victorious conclusion of human history – 'as the waters cover the sea'.

Seven

A Song of Praise – Glory, Not Grumbling

Habakkuk 3:1–19

The basic argument of the book is now complete. Habakkuk has finished his complaints against God and what is happening all around him. No longer does he feel that God sits idly by while Judah, the very people of God, wallows in violence and evil. Then his second argument with God finds its answer too. How could a holy God use the shockingly evil and godless Babylonians as his instruments? Surely this contradicts the fundamental nature of God as the holy one of Israel. But chapter two with its series of woes reveals how God's judgments vindicate his absolute holiness, ultimately he reigns 'in his holy temple' (2:20) and the knowledge of his glory will triumph in all the world. Habakkuk's debate with God ends therefore in the prophet being reduced to silence before the Lord. When God declares his purposes and shows his hand in sovereign power, all human grumblings and complaints come to an end. As Job also experienced at the end of his sufferings, dialogue with God can only finally end in our reverent silence.

So the book of Habakkuk teaches us that it may be good to voice our questioning objections to misfortunes that befall us or to tragedy which surrounds us in our fallen world. So often our circumstances seem to go against all that we believe concerning God, and we cannot make sense of what is happening to us and all around us. Habakkuk could not reconcile God's apparent inactivity and then his use of the Babylonians as his instruments with God's total holiness. But finally his and our complaints will come to their inevitable conclusion. When God shows us himself in all his glory and justice, we can only bow before him in awe-filled worship. His ways are indeed perfect in love and sinlessly holy. He is the Lord over history and over the movements of the nations of the world. And his justice walks hand-in-hand with his grace.

So the prophet ends his book with a song of praise and worship. His song is in the form of a prayer (3:1) which is probably set to music.[1] We are not surprised therefore that this chapter has formed the basis for a modern cantata by György Kósa. Keil in his commentary suggests that the word *shigionoth* was 'applied to the giddiness both of intoxication and of love'. The prayer in this chapter is then no dreary dirge, but rather it moves with poetry and excitement. With such a prayer there is no fear of yawning with boredom!

Verse two summarizes the contents of this chapter. Habakkuk remembers all that God is in his essential nature, his fame in all the world and all that he has done. Then he prays that God will act in the same way now in his day, working in such a way that what God does should become known. Today we also long that God's saving work may become the gossip in the public arena and the content of the media. So it was in the area of Indonesia where my wife and I worked. The work of

Christ in changing multitudes of lives was indeed the talk of the town.

In 3:3–15 therefore Habakkuk reminds himself and his readers of God's splendour and mighty working in the past. In chapter two the main emphasis had been on the wrath of God in righteous judgment with just the slight relief of the glorious promise in 2:14. But now the prophet prays that in his wrath the Lord will remember mercy (3:2). And in the concluding verses of chapter three Habakkuk works up to a triumphant climax of confident rejoicing in the sovereign Lord's enabling grace and power. May our prayers too find their conclusion in similar assured faith in the living God! We rejoice in God's amazing mercy.

Like many more liberal critics, Adam Smith rejects the idea that God could show wrath, for his emphasis is more on the loving kindness of the Lord. So he declares that the use of the word 'wrath' misses the point, rightly showing that actually the word means 'turmoil'. This is no cool calculated attitude of disfavour, but rather a passionately emotional anger against sin. In his book *A Theology of the Pain of God*, Kitamori expounds Jeremiah 31:20 and underlines the fact that God's heart 'yearns'. The Hebrew word *chamah* is a strongly emotional word of suffering which is also used of decapitated chickens fluttering wildly around the yard before finally dying. It is also used of waves crashing on the seashore with their water splashing powerfully all over the place. God is no unemotional robot administering judgment without being personally involved. We see this supremely in the suffering of Christ in bearing the penalty for all our sin in his body on the cross. The Father himself suffered together with his beloved Son in Jesus' sacrificial death.

So the previous chapter clearly demonstrates the reality of God's just and fearful judgment. Nevertheless, the prophet now pleads with God to remember mercy and to pour out his unexpected and undeserved love to people who deserve nothing but judgment. This is the glorious grace of which Paul speaks when he says that 'while we were still sinners Christ died for us' and that 'Christ died for the ungodly' (Rom. 5:8; Rom. 5:6). In the brilliant light of such mercy it is no wonder that Habakkuk sings his prayer of rejoicing. All his questioning complaints give way to the strains of exuberant praise.

The mighty working of God (3:3–7)

In this section the prophet follows the common biblical pattern of looking back in history to some of the great things the Lord had done for his people Israel. It is often good for us to remember past glories when God has shown his grace and power in granting us special favours and helping us in very particular ways. In this way we may gain strengthened reassurance that God will also work on our behalf in the present and on into the future. Strong faith is thus built on the foundation of the memory of past demonstrations of God's love.

The language used in these verses strikes us particularly vividly because the verb forms are mainly indicating things that are happening in the present or even in the future. Traditional Jewish thought differs from the usual European way of thinking, and therefore also in its verb forms. It does not generally relate to the division of events into the past, present and future. As Jews we feel ourselves intimately bound up with the history of our forefathers and also with the as yet unseen future. As contemporary people we play our part in the unfolding development of our people, our society and family from one generation to another.

So it is, for example, in the Lord's Supper that we are personally identified with the past exodus from Egypt, the return from exile in Babylon, the cross of Jesus the Messiah and the future Messianic banquet at the table of Abraham. Past, present and future roll into one. We don't just remember with some trick of the mind, but we are actually associated with those events, we are part of them. Likewise when Paul says that we have been crucified, buried and resurrected with Christ, he means what he says. We have died together with Jesus on the cross, been buried with him in the coldness of the tomb and been raised to new life with him in his resurrection. And Paul even uses the present tense when he declares that we *are* seated with Christ in heavenly places (Eph. 2:6). The ascension of Jesus is already a present reality for us and we eagerly look forward to its climactic fullness when we shall be fully in glory with the Lord.

Habakkuk therefore brings the past events in the history of Israel right into the present, reminding himself and his readers that we experience these works of saving grace now in today's world. And these sovereign actions of God in history live on into the future, so we can rejoice in God's assured goodness as we stride confidently into the coming days and years.

But the English language has difficulty in expressing this merging of past, present and future, so our Bibles translate the verbs of this passage as if they were in the past tense – 'God *came* from Teman' and so on. Clearly Habakkuk is referring back to Deuteronomy 33:2 and God's glory coming down from Mount Paran in the giving of the Law through Moses. It would seem that Teman and Paran represent the start and the conclusion of Israel's wanderings through the wilderness en route to the Promised Land of Canaan. God's presence accompanied the people of Israel from the exodus from Egypt and the giving of the Law right through into their promised destination. So now as Habakkuk looks into the future, the vision that God's revelation will certainly come (2:3) is fulfilled. Not only does God's revelation *come* to light, but God himself in all his glory *comes*. God always takes the initiative in moving towards us in his loving grace, longing to enter into intimate relationship with us.

In 3:3–7 Habakkuk refers to God in the third person, while in verses 8–15 he progresses to direct speech in addressing God and therefore moves into the second person 'you'. When talking about God Habakkuk uses the name *Eloah*, the singular form of *Elohim*. This name relates particularly to the creation in the first two chapters of Genesis. Likewise the word 'earth' reminds the reader of the fact that God created the heavens and *the earth*. In the Bible the fact of creation stands as the evidence that God rules over all peoples and all things everywhere, not just the people and land of Israel. God created the whole earth and all that is in it, so all belongs to him. The creation is the beginning of *human* history, not just of Israel's history. We are therefore not surprised that in 3:6 it is not only Israel which trembles before the glory and might of God, but also 'the nations'. The book of Habakkuk assumes this truth that God rules over all the nations of the world, not just over his covenant people Israel. And in the New Testament we see how the Jewish Messiah Jesus welcomes Gentiles of every nation and people as his followers. The saving gospel of Jesus reaches out to all nations and the church becomes a multinational entity. International mission is therefore central to the biblical revelation of God's purposes for all humanity.

In verse three therefore, Habakkuk declares that God's glory extends throughout the heavens and the whole earth, proceeding then to affirm the absolute power of God's glory. In the New Testament too Paul's letter to the Colossians reaffirms the same great truth that the glory of God in Jesus Christ relates not only to all humanity, but also to all creation. Paul underlines this with his repeated 'all things' in Colossians 1:15–20. So we are reminded both of the extent and the might of God's glory.

With its reference to Sinai and the giving of the Law verse three brings together the universal fact of God's creation and the more particular reality of God's covenant with Israel. It is so important to keep these two inseparably together. If we emphasize God's universal creation to the neglect of his particular relationship with Israel, we may be tempted to fall into universalism with no distinction between God's people and the rest of the world. But if we overemphasize God's gracious election of his people to be his chosen ones, we can easily become a select little spiritual ghetto rejoicing in our own salvation with little concern for the world God created.

The allusion to Sinai and the giving of the Law relates closely to the fact that God is 'the Holy One' (3:3) as we also saw in 1:12. Because God is entirely holy, therefore he demands in his Law that his people should also live holy lives. As we have seen already, this insistence on holiness and ethical purity as a condition for any living relationship with God lies at the very heart of the biblical revelation. No other religion can parallel the centrality of this truth.

When God revealed the Law at Sinai, his glory descended on his people. Israel was astonished to see the light of God's glory shining on Moses' skin as he came down from the mountain. It may be that the second half of Habakkuk 3:4 is referring to this when it says that 'rays flashed from his hand', for it is here the same basic word as in Exodus 34:29,30,35 where Moses' face was *'radiant* because he had spoken with the Lord'. Likewise Habakkuk goes on to say that God's 'power was hidden', a reminder of how Moses 'put a veil over his face' (Ex. 34:33) to hide God's glory reflected on his skin. God's burning purity and splendour are too glorious for mere humans to face. But wonderfully in 2 Corinthians 3:7–18 Paul tells us that the veil is removed so that we can now behold the glory of the Lord. Thanks to the redeeming work of Christ we can now come boldly into the full presence of the glorious and holy God. Indeed we are even being changed into his likeness from one degree of glory to another.

In chapter one the Babylonians seemed to be irresistible in their terrible destructive march as they conquered nation after nation. Now it is God himself whose victorious march passes through the world with absolute power. Glory, praise and splendour fill the earth, rays flash from his hand. Fearful judgment precedes him and follows after him, plague goes before him and pestilence follows his footsteps. Even when he stops his march through the lands and stands still (3:6) the earth shakes and the nations tremble. Seemingly immovable mountains crumble into nothing before him and the age-old hills just collapse. Great mountains dominate the scenery and impress us with their grandeur, but actually they are as nothing compared with the might of God. The mountains and hills seem to last forever, but in reality it is God's ways which are eternal (3:6). In this we are further reminded of 1:12 in which the prophet begins his second complaint with the affirmation that God's ways are 'from everlasting'. Empires and nations rise and fall, but God remains steadfastly in command.

Some six hundred years later Zechariah, John the Baptist's father, sang from the same song-sheet as

Habakkuk, glorying in God's 'salvation from our enemies and from the hand of all who hate us' (Lk. 1:71). In Habakkuk 3:7 Cushan and Midian represent the nations and peoples who harried and attacked Israel in their wilderness wanderings and in their early years in the Promised Land. So the culmination of the prophet's descriptions of God's glorious power is his deliverance of Israel from these enemies who caused them so much trouble. No longer would it be Israel which would suffer, but distress would come upon 'the tents of Cushan' and anguish upon 'the dwellings of Midian'. God's holy justice prevails.

This verse in Habakkuk is the only biblical reference to Cushan, but it is probable that Cushan-Rishathaim (Judg. 3:8), king of Mesopotamia, relates to the same area. It would seem that Cushan-Rishathaim was the first to defeat and subjugate Israel after their arrival in Canaan. Israel had sinned against the Lord and done evil in his sight, so Cushan became the instrument in the hands of God. God's 'anger burned against Israel' and they became subject to Cushan for eight years before the Lord 'raised up for them a deliverer' (Judg. 3:8–9).

Again 'the Israelites did evil in the eyes of the Lord' and as a result 'for seven years he gave them into the hands of the Midianites' (Judg. 6:1). But then in Judges 7 God raises up Gideon to deliver Israel from her oppressors. In a song of rejoicing Isaiah too glories in God's defeat of Midian (Is. 9:4) as an example of the Lord's wonderful acts of deliverance. God has given Israel abundant joy which is underlined by the threefold repetition of the word 'rejoice' in Isaiah 9:3. Was this passage also in Habakkuk's mind when he determined to 'rejoice in the Lord' and to 'be joyful in God my Saviour' (3:18)? But Isaiah also widens the scope of God's saving work to include 'the people walking in darkness', those who are

outside God's covenant promises and the light of his
Law (Is. 9:2). The New Testament will pick up on this
theme of the light shining in the Gentile darkness (e.g.
Jn. 1:5) and quoting Isaiah Matthew will glory in the fact
that 'the people living in darkness have seen a great
light' (Mt. 4:16). This is in the context of 'Galilee of the
Gentiles' and the coming of the kingdom of heaven
which extends throughout the world, not just among
God's people. Jew and Gentile together are included in
God's redemption in Jesus Christ. We notice again how
the universality of God's purposes is central to the biblical revelation – and must therefore also be central to the
life and faith of all followers of Jesus Christ.

It is noteworthy that Isaiah's rejoicing in God shatter-
ing the oppressive Midianites leads on to his prophecy
concerning the coming of the Messiah. That is the context of 'unto us a child is born, unto us a son is given, and
the government will be on his shoulders. And he will be
called Wonderful Counsellor, Mighty God, Everlasting
Father, Prince of Peace' (Is. 9:6). Habakkuk rejoices too
that God has delivered and will deliver his people from
the judgment of God and the oppression of Cushan and
the Midianites, but he does not specifically declare that
God's deliverance will come through the person of the
Messiah.

The prophet addresses the Lord directly (3:8–15)

In the Old Testament times Israel tended to look on the
sea as something threatening and frightening. The forces
of the waves seemed angry and beyond human control,
and there was always a danger that enemies might suddenly and unexpectedly appear in boats to attack them.
In their book *The Message of Mission* Howard Peskett and

Vinoth Ramachandra observe that 'The sea represents, both in the Old Testament and in Revelation, the chaotic power of anticreation, the primeval abyss which constantly threatens to engulf the earth and humanity. Always restless, it is a symbol of all those forces that attempt to undo God's moral order.'[2]

But Habakkuk in his direct words to the Lord affirms his faith in the Lord's ultimate control even over the waters. As the Psalmist declares, 'Mightier than the thunder of the great waters, mightier than the breakers of the sea – the Lord on high is mighty' (Ps. 93:4). And Jesus demonstrates this by commanding fearsome waves to be still, so that his disciples note with awe that 'Even the wind and the waves obey him!' (Mk. 4:41). In Habakkuk 3:8 the great rivers lay beneath the power of God's anger. Were these the rivers on which Cushan was located? Did God's wrath extend to these mighty streams of water? In asking this question Habakkuk remembers the power of God which divided the waters of the Red Sea as Israel escaped from the pursuing armies of Egypt. And in the original creation God demonstrated his power in causing rivers to separate one area of land from another. He has such overwhelming power that even the mountains writhe in turmoil before him. Torrents of water obey his commands, lifting their waves on high rather than allowing them to crash down and break into swirling masses of water.

Habakkuk goes on to remember that God had allowed Israel to 'avenge itself on its enemies' (Josh. 10:13) by causing the sun to stand still in the sky and the moon to halt its progress. So Habakkuk reinforces his faith in God's gracious deliverance, 'surely the Lord was fighting for Israel!' (Josh. 10:14). The prophet looks forward to God's mighty salvation for Habakkuk himself and for the people of Israel. Today we too can share in that same confident faith in the mighty deliverance of God in whatever trials and battles we may face. He fights for us! And what a graphic portrayal of God's mighty deeds Habakkuk gives us! The glint of God's flying arrows, the lightning of his flashing spear, God striding through the earth in wrath and threshing the nations in his anger!

Habakkuk's words make us tremble as we see the fearful danger of opposing God and his people. Finally God will never allow his name to be dragged in the mud nor his people to be put down. He 'crushes the leader of the land of wickedness' and 'strips him from head to foot', 'with his own spear you pierced his head'. And the climax relates again to God's power over the waters of the sea: 'you trampled the sea with your horses, churning the great waters' (3:15).

In our modern, more comfortable age we find it difficult to contemplate the power of a holy God in dynamic action. We may react against the whole idea of God 'crushing' people or violently destroying them. Even God's sovereign power over the forces of nature seems to contradict our environmental concerns. But 3:13 puts all these matters into their right context. God's great purpose is 'to deliver his people' and 'to save his anointed one'. The Lord acts not only to vindicate his own holiness and justice, but particularly in loving grace he also longs to bring his salvation to his much loved people. God's purpose to bring salvation to the world burns so brightly in his heart that he will go to such lengths. And we see the outworking of this in the fact that God was willing even to send his son to earth to suffer and die for our salvation. He was willing even to pay such a price for the deliverance of his people.

In 3:13 we notice 'your anointed one'. Habakkuk uses here the word for 'Messiah'. God called his people Israel to act as his means of salvation for all nations, but sadly sin prevailed and generally they proved unworthy of God's high calling. But God in his grace brought deliverance to his anointed people. God sent his son Jesus to be the perfect son of Abraham, the perfect Israelite. Jesus fulfilled Israel's high Messianic calling of achieving salvation and deliverance for the world. He is the perfect 'anointed one'. Then the followers of Jesus, both Jews and Gentiles, take over that same Messianic baton. As God's anointed ones, we continue to run the race to bring God's salvation to the world. So we see a glorious continuity: Israel as God's chosen people – Jesus, the perfect Messiah and the perfect son of Abraham – God's international church which consists now both of Jews and Gentiles. We are God's anointed people, called to the Messianic ministry of bringing Jesus Christ's salvation and deliverance to our needy world.

Rejoicing in God's saving work, we are not surprised by the title for God which Habakkuk uses. He addresses God as *Yhwh* (3:8), the warmly personal name which relates to the covenant. But even in the comforting use of the covenantal name *Yhwh* we cannot separate his work of gracious deliverance (3:12) from its surrounding context of fearful judgment and wrath against those who 'scatter' God's beloved people and 'gloat' over their misfortunes. The wrath of the holy God stands together with his loving grace towards his elect. The fearful judgment of God and his gracious work of salvation represent the two sides of the one coin.

The climax – Habakkuk's confident faith (3:16–19)

Although Habakkuk normally emphasizes the fact that the word of the Lord is to be *seen*, here he states that he has *heard* (compare 3:2) the Lord's answer to all his complaints. He doubtless has in mind the fearful judgments of chapter two and perhaps also the descriptions of God's power in action in 3:2–15. As a result of hearing God's word concerning his irresistible might and the outworking of his holiness and justice, Habakkuk is overwhelmed both physically and emotionally. His heart pounded, his lips quivered, his bones crumbled in decay and he trembled from beneath (this could indicate some sort of earth tremble beneath him or it could mean that his legs, the lower part of his body, trembled).

We may note the double use of the word 'tremble' in this verse. His heart and his legs *trembled*. The same word, *ragaz*, is translated as 'stand in awe' in 3:2 and it comes again in 3:7. The prophet trembles when he hears of God's wrath and his mighty deeds. Israel's enemies also tremble before the power of God. The same word is used, for example, in Deuteronomy 2:25 and Isaiah 64:2. Not only Israel, but also the surrounding Gentile nations will tremble at the very presence of God, and when they hear reports of his victorious working on behalf of his people. In Psalm 77:18, Isaiah 5:25 and Amos 8:8 we may observe that it is not only people who tremble before the Lord, but also nature itself – the earth, the hills and the land *tremble* because of God's righteous judgment against sin and injustice. God will not forget Israel's materialism, dishonesty and unjust oppression of the poor and needy (Amos 8:7), so the land will tremble and its inhabitants will mourn. In Job 39:24 the same word refers to the 'frenzied excitement' of a war horse. So Habakkuk seeks to describe how strong emotional reactions overcame him as he heard God's word and as he waited patiently for a day of calamity to come on the invading armies of the Babylonians.

The NIV faces us with a marked contrast in the following words 'Yet I will wait patiently . . .' The connecting word is better translated as 'because', the reason why the prophet is so overcome. Not only has he heard of God's overwhelmingly powerful judgment, but also he has to wait patiently for the inevitable day of judgment which will come upon the Babylonians. He knows what God has declared. The Babylonians will invade Judah and destroy them, but then a day of calamity will assail them in their turn. The mighty hand of almighty God will be stretched out first against Judah and then against the Babylonians. No wonder Habakkuk is reduced to awestruck silence!

The NIV translation '*the* day of calamity' sounds like an eschatological reference to the final Day of Judgment. But a better translation would avoid the definite article here, for Habakkuk merely observes that he is waiting patiently for '*a* day of calamity'. Such a day is foreordained and unavoidable. It may also foreshadow the final great day of the Lord, the day of final judgment. But the day of the Babylonians' judgment does not coincide with that end-time day. As David Baker writes in his Tyndale commentary, it is 'but an anticipatory representation of what the final Day will be, a guarantee of its coming and an indication of its character . . .'

In the twenty-first century it is easy to concentrate so much on the positive grace of God in our salvation and resurrection life that we ignore the negative truth of God's fearful judgment. As a result we may find the experience of the prophet largely alien to us. Words of judgment both in the Old Testament and in the New Testament do not move us with that same horror as we patiently await that inevitable day when God will vindicate his righteousness and sin will reap its just consequences. We need to learn afresh the seriousness of sin and allow the fearful reality of God's just judgment to impact on us as it did with Habakkuk. No longer is the prophet afflicted with doubts and complaints against God, for the Lord's prophetic words fully support Habakkuk's faith in the holiness of God (compare 1:12,13; 2:20; 3:3). His grumbles are silenced and he is overwhelmed by God's word to him.

In our day too we are assailed by the horrors of what is happening in the world around us. Human trafficking, AIDS, wars, terrorism and holocausts fill our news broadcasts. Evil and injustice seem to prevail uncontrollably. How good therefore to follow the model of Habakkuk, who somehow combined patient waiting for God's day of judgment with the highly emotional symptoms of a pounding heart and trembling limbs.

Habakkuk had also grown well beyond his previous attitude of complaining against the Lord because of his own and his people's situations. Judah still suffers deprivation and hunger, but no longer does the prophet put the blame on God. It remains true that the fig tree bears no fruit, the vines have no grapes and the sheep and cattle have vanished from the land. Hunger and even starvation must have threatened the people, for they depended on their annual agriculture. They were subsistence farmers and a year of failed crops and cattle dying from lack of rain spelled disaster. Even now in modern times we know the dreadful reality of such famine situations, for we have all seen pictures of such tragedy on our TV screens even if we have never experienced such suffering ourselves.

But Habakkuk has now learned in the midst even of such a situation to rejoice in the Lord (3:18) and somehow to be 'joyful in God my Saviour'. In such circumstances rejoicing and joyfulness seem almost out of place. But the prophet has come to appreciate where true joy is to be found. It does not stem from outward circumstances. Habakkuk's joy is in the Lord himself, in God who is his Saviour.

How easy it is to slip into the materialism of our age, in which we rejoice in the comforts of home, exotic holidays, materialistic acquisitions in a consumerist society and other outward things. But deep joy can only be found in our relationship with God, our trust in him, our grateful enjoyment of his gracious love for us whatever our outward circumstances.

My mind returns to an old leprosy sufferer in North Sumatera, Indonesia. The disease had eaten away his hands and feet. He was blind and without ears or nose. In the dingy poverty of a leprosy colony ward he brandished his handless arms before my face and declared how happy he was to have been allowed to suffer from leprosy, because it was in the leprosy colony that he had come to know the Lord. Like the prophet, he was rejoicing in the Lord and in the sure reality that God was his Saviour. He told me with obvious delight that after forty-five years of leprosy he would surely soon be with the Lord in glory. I often remember this man when tempted to complain about my relatively minor difficulties.

In 3:18 we may observe that Habakkuk's rejoicing is in *Yhwh*, the covenant name which signifies the Lord's gracious relationship with his people. In situations of famine people may seem to be so sadly worthless, but *Yhwh's* love never abandons them and flows around them even in the worst of circumstances. Apparently insignificant or worthless human beings are given deep value and worth by the fact that God has chosen to relate intimately with us in his covenant. In the second half of the verse the prophet's use of the name *Yhwh* is further fortified by adding the title *Elohim*, the sovereign creator God. The gracious covenant *Yhwh* is also the almighty

God who is sovereign over the very creation which seems to have fallen into chaos and disorder. He is the Saviour. He not only desires to save his people, but also has the total power to do so. He is the Creator of all the earth.

The prophet has faced the sad reality of Judah's sin despite her calling as the covenantal people of God. Then God confronted him with his perplexing plan to raise up the immensely cruel and idolatrous Babylonians as his means of judging Judah. Nothing seemed to make sense in the light of Habakkuk's assured faith in the Lord as the holy one of Israel. What God allowed and what he actually did seemed clearly contradictory to the very nature of God in his holiness. No wonder Habakkuk resorted to complaining strongly and blaming God. Surely God understood and sympathized with the prophet's weakness in this. As a result the Lord revealed to Habakkuk his ultimate plans. He would judge the Babylonians for their barbaric cruelty and evil. His holiness and justice would be demonstrated to all concerned. He would at the same time cause the whole earth to be filled with the knowledge of his glory. All people in every part of the world will see that the Lord alone is perfect in his splendour. Sovereignly, God declares that he is 'in his holy temple' (2:20) where he is not only present in the midst of his people, but also reigns supreme in his absolute glory. So it is not only the people of Judah who are commanded to keep silence in his presence, but 'all the earth' is to be struck dumb before the majesty of almighty God. The whole earth, all the peoples of the world, will 'be filled with the knowledge of the glory of the Lord' (2:14) and likewise 'all the earth' will now bow before him, unable to voice their complaints or boastings any more. And Habakkuk himself joins in that Job-like silence.

Habakkuk has now not only learned to find the source of his rejoicing and heartfelt joy in the Lord himself, but he also finds that his strength too comes from the Lord. Habakkuk has no strength within himself – decay has afflicted his bones and his legs tremble in wobbling weakness (3:16). But he finds renewed strength in *Yhwh Adonai*, the Lord *Yhwh*, 'the Sovereign Lord'. Throughout the centuries the people of God have found comfort, joy and new strength through this wonderful verse. 'He makes my feet like the feet of a deer, he enables me to go on the heights'. Whatever our circumstances and whatever is happening in the world around us we can skip along the steep heights of the mountainside with the agility and strength of a mountain deer.

Habakkuk's outward circumstances have not changed at all. But no longer does he resort to complaining or blaming God for all the fearful sin and evil he is witnessing. Now he can trust in the Lord's total holiness and the perfection of his purposes. He finds renewed joy in the Lord himself and confidently asserts that God is 'my Saviour' (3:18). Christians can rejoice in the Lord himself with even greater confidence, for we know that God has brought the fullness of salvation to us through Jesus Christ. Because of his atoning sacrifice on the cross and life-giving resurrection we believe with assurance that he is in fullness 'my Saviour'.

So this little book of Habakkuk comes to its joyful conclusion. And the final words show that the prophet's words in chapter three are meant to be sung with the beauty of 'stringed instruments'. As we read the book of Habakkuk may we also go out into our tragically evil and idolatrous world with such a song in our hearts and such confident faith in the Lord that the multitudes of this world may see the reality of our God and his wonderful purposes! As Paul declared (Rom. 12:2), God's will is 'good, pleasing and perfect' – and there is nothing better than perfect.

So no more complaints! No more blaming God! Rejoice in the Lord!

Bibliography

Baker, David W., *Nahum, Habakkuk and Zephaniah* (Westmont: Inter-Varsity Press, 1988).

Barker, Kenneth L. and Waylon Bailey, *The New American Commentary on Micah, Nahum, Habakkuk and Zephaniah* (Nashville: Broadman and Holman, 1999).

Barth, Karl, *Church Dogmatics* (London: T & T Clark, 2004).

Ben-Gurion, David, *Recollections* (American Fork: Covenant Communications Corporation, 1970).

Botterweck G.J. and H. Ringgren (eds.), *Theologisches Wörterbuch zum Alten Testament* (Stuttgart: W. Kohlhammer, 1970).

Brown, Francis, Samuel Driver and Charles Briggs, *Brown, Driver and Briggs Hebrew and English Lexicon* (Peabody: Hendrickson Publishers, 1996).

Calvin, John, *Commentary on Habakkuk*.

Davidson, A.B. (ed.), *The Books of Nahum, Habakkuk and Zephaniah* (Cambridge: Cambridge University Press, 1905).

Douglas, J.D. (ed.) *New Bible Dictionary* (Westmont: Inter-Varsity Press, 1982).

Dunn, James D.G., *Word Biblical Commentary: Volume 38A, Romans 1–8* (Nashville: Thomas Nelson, 1988).

Eissfeldt, O., *The Old Testament, An Introduction* (New York: Harper and Row, 1965).

Ellicott, C.J. (ed.), *A Bible Commentary for English Readers* (London: Cassell and Company).

Ellison, H.L., *Men Spake From God* (Exeter: Paternoster, 1952).

Goldsmith, Elizabeth, *God Can Be Trusted* (Carlisle: OM Publishing/Authentic Media, 2003).

Goldsmith, Martin, *Habakkuk and Joel: God is Sovereign in History* (London: Marshall, Morgan and Scott, 1982).

Goldsmith, Martin, *Jesus and his Relationships* (Carlisle: Paternoster, 2000).

Goldsmith, Martin, *Get a Grip on Mission, the Challenge of a Changing World* (Westmont: Inter-Varsity Press, 2006).

Goldsmith, Martin, *Good News for All Nations: Mission at the Heart of the New Testament* (London: Hodder & Stoughton, 2002).

Goldsmith, Martin, *What About Other Faiths?* (London: Hodder & Stoughton, 2002).

Goldsmith, Martin, *Life's Tapestry* (Carlisle: Authentic Media, 1997).

Harris, R. Laird, Gleason L. Archer Jr. and Bruce K. Waltke, *Theological Wordbook of the Old Testament* (Chicago: Moody Publishers, 1980).

House, P.R., *The Unity of the Twelve* (Sheffield: Almond Press, 1990).

Jöcken, P., *Das Buch Habakuk* (Bonn: Peter Hanstein, 1977).

Keil, C.F. and F. Delitzsch, *Commentary on the Old Testament* (Grand Rapids: Eerdmans, 1980).

Kitamori, K., *Theology of the Pain of God* (Richmond: John Knox Press, 1965).

Koyama, Kosuke, *Three Mile An Hour God: Biblical Reflections* (New York: Orbis Books, 1980).

Mason, Rex, *Zephaniah, Habakkuk, Joel* (Sheffield: Sheffield Academic Press, 1994).

Peskett, Howard, and Vinoth Ramachandra, *The Message of Mission* (Westmont: Inter-Varsity Press, 2003).

Prior, David, *The Message of Joel, Micah & Habakkuk* (Westmont: Inter-Varsity Press, 1998).

Robertson, O. Palmer, *The New International Commentary on the Old Testament: the Books of Nahum, Habakkuk and Zephaniah* (Grand Rapids: Eerdmans, 1990).

Wright, Christopher J.H., *The Mission of God: Unlocking the Bible's Grand Narrative* (Westmont: Inter-Varsity Press, 2006).

Endnotes

Foreword

[1] Martin Goldsmith, *Habakkuk and Joel: God is Sovereign in History*.

Introduction

[1] See O. Palmer Robertson, *The New International Commentary on the Old Testament: The Books of Nahum, Habakkuk and Zephaniah*.

[2] Kenneth L. Barker and Waylon Bailey, *The New American Commentary: Micah, Nahum, Habakkuk, Zephaniah*.

[3] Josiah reigned in Judah from 640–609 BC and the Book of the Law was found in 622/1 BC.

[4] Rex Mason in *Zephaniah, Habakkuk, Joel* observes 'Since their military methods and ferocity seem to be known, it is reasonable to suppose that this oracle at least originated in the period of Neo-Babylonian imperial expansion'.

[5] For a good description of the basic outline of the chronology of the time see J.D. Douglas (ed.) *New Bible Dictionary*. For further study of the dating of Habakkuk, and therefore the context in which he was writing, see any larger commentary on Habakkuk – for example Robertson, *Nahum*,

Habakkuk and Zephaniah. For a major study of previous scholarship related to Habakkuk see P. Jöcken, *Das Buch Habakuk.*

6 Surprisingly, however, the *New Bible Dictionary* dates Habakkuk 'at the close of the seventh century BC shortly after the battle of Carchemish'.

One – Habakkuk's First Complaint

1 In R. Laird Harris, Gleason L. Archer Jr. and Bruce K. Waltke, *Theological Wordbook of the Old Testament*, p. 601.

2 For further study of the use of the word in this sense see G.J.Botterweck and H.Ringgren (eds.) *Theologisches Wörterbuch zum Alten Testament.*

3 David Ben-Gurion, *Recollections.*

4 *Chazah* comes in 1:1; 2:1; 3:7,10. The common word for 'to see', *raah*, comes in 1:3,13; 3:6, *nabat* in 1:5,13 (twice); 2:5. It should be noted that the Hebrew *nabat* is etymologically different from the word for a prophet (*nabi*), but the sounds are related and therefore remind the reader of the fact that Habakkuk is called 'Habakkuk the prophet' (1:1; 3:1).

5 See Robertson, *Nahum, Habakkuk, Zephaniah.*

6 Harris, Archer and Waltke, *Theological Wordbook.*

7 It is interesting in this context that the prophets sometimes replace the name *'Bethel'*, the House of God, with the derogatory title *'Bethaven'*, the House of Iniquity (e.g. Hos. 5:8; 10:5). This occurs in the context of rank idolatry.

8 The verb for 'to see' (*raah*) is in the Hiphil tense and therefore has the sense of 'cause to see'.

9 See Barker and Bailey, *Micah, Nahum, Habakkuk, Zephaniah.*

10 For this combination see Isaiah 16:4; 22:4; Jeremiah 6:7; 20:8; 48:3; Ezekiel 45:9.

11 For further discussion of this topic see M. Goldsmith, *Jesus and his Relationships.*

[12] Ben-Gurion, *Recollections*.

[13] Some commentators (such as Ewald and König) have suggested that the wicked in 1:2–4 are not the people of Judah, but the Assyrians who oppressed God's people and were themselves to be destroyed in their turn by the Babylonians (see also O. Eissfeldt, *The Old Testament, An Introduction*). But the context of the whole message of Habakkuk would seem to indicate that these verses relate to Judah. Calvin in his commentary on Habakkuk states that 'as the prophet addresses the Jews . . . There is no doubt but that he refers to them.' Likewise, H.L. Ellison in his *Men Spake From God* affirms that 'the most natural interpretation is that the prophet is complaining about internal troubles'.

[14] Mason, *Zephaniah, Habakkuk, Joel*.

[15] P.R. House, *The Unity of the Twelve*.

[16] For stories of testimony concerning answered prayer in the lives of my wife and myself see Elizabeth Goldsmith, *God Can Be Trusted*.

Two – God's Shocking Answer

[1] For further discussion of this theme see Martin Goldsmith, *Get a Grip on Mission, the Challenge of a Changing World*.

[2] For further exposition of Luke's concern for God's work among the Gentiles see Martin Goldsmith, *Good News for All Nations: Mission at the Heart of the New Testament*.

[3] David Prior, *The Message of Joel, Micah and Habakkuk*.

[4] Harris, Gleason and Waltke, *Theological Wordbook*.

[5] Goldsmith, *Habakkuk and Joel*.

[6] The clause 'Their hordes advance like a desert wind' is very unclear in the Hebrew. For a brief but good summary of the textual problem see David W. Baker, *Nahum, Habakkuk and Zephaniah*.

Three – Habakkuk's Second Complaint

[1] Despite having suffered in a Japanese prison camp in China as a girl and then faced many trials in her experiences as a missionary in Asia, my wife has called her autobiography *God Can Be Trusted*.

[2] For further reference to the biblical names for the creator and their significance in the context of the Christian understanding of other faiths, see Martin Goldsmith, *What About Other Faiths?*

Four – How Will God Answer?

[1] In C.J. Ellicott (ed.), *A Bible Commentary for English Readers*.

[2] See also Goldsmith, *Good News for All Nations*.

Five – God's Solution

[1] K. Kitamori, *A Theology of the Pain of God*.

[2] In the Piel form of the verb it can also have the sense of 'finish' or 'cut off'. Was the prophet suggesting that what they were coveting was actually going to be brought to an ignominious end?

[3] Habakkuk uses a different Hebrew word from that in Ecclesiastes, but the meaning is the same.

[4] Christopher J.H. Wright, *The Mission of God – Unlocking the Bible's Grand Narrative*.

Six – Filled With the Knowledge of His Glory

[1] The Greek word for 'church' (*ekklesia*) is the translation in the Septuagint, the Greek translation of the Old Testament, for the 'congregation' (*qahal*) of Israel.

Seven – A Song of Praise

[1] *On Shigionoth*, as the NIV note states, is probably a musical term (see also Ps. 7:1).

[2] Howard Peskett and Vinoth Ramachandra, *The Message of Mission*.